Photoshop® 7 Power Shortcuts

W9-BPN-066

PHOTOSHOP®7
POWER
SHORTCUTS

MICHAEL NINNESS

201 West 103rd Street, Indianapolis, Indiana 46290

An Imprint of Pearson Education

Boston • Indianapolis • London • Munich • New York • San Francisco

New Riders

Photoshop 7 Power Shortcuts

International Standard Book Number: 0-7357-1331-6

Library of Congress Catalog Card Number: 2002115354

Printed in the United States of America

First edition: January 2003

07 06 05 04 03   7 6 5 4 3 2 1

Interpretation of the printing code: The rightmost double-digit number is the year of the book's printing; the rightmost single-digit number is the number of the book's printing. For example, the printing code 03-1 shows that the first printing of the book occurred in 2003.

Trademarks

Warning and Disclaimer

Publisher
David Dwyer

Associate Publisher
Stephanie Wall

Editor in Chief
Chris Nelson

Executive Editor
Steve Weiss

Production Manager
Gina Kanouse

Senior Product Marketing Manager
Tammy Detrich

Publicity Manager
Susan Nixon

Senior Editor
Sarah Kearns

Project Editor
Kelley Thornton

Senior Indexer
Cheryl Lenser

Composition
Gloria Schurick

Manufacturing Coordinator
Dan Uhrig

Cover Designer
Aren Howell

Contents

The 15 Tips You Must Learn. Quicker. 1

Palettes 5

Contents

Contents

Contents

Contents

About the Author

Michael Ninness is a product manager at Microsoft. Prior to this, he spent three years with Adobe Systems Incorporated as the LiveMotion group product manager. Before joining Adobe, he was the group product manager for the Photoshop plug-ins and imaging products at Extensis Corporation. He has spent the last 12 years as a graphic designer, instructor, author, and computer graphics guru. Michael is the conference chair for the Professional Photoshop Conference at Macworld Conference and Expo. He is a featured speaker at other events such as Internet World, Comdex, and the Photoshop and Web Design World conferences produced by Thunder Lizard Productions. He is also the author of *Photoshop 5 Web Magic* and has been a contributor to *Photoshop User* and *Design Graphics* magazines.

About the Contributor

John Nack is a Photoshop product manager at Adobe Systems Incorporated. John joined the Photoshop team after serving as LiveMotion Product Manager, where he was responsible for managing the program's design and animation features. Prior to working at Adobe, John was a designer and animator at AGENCY.COM New York, where he created web sites for clients such as Gucci™, Coca-Cola™, Nike™, and British Airways™.

About the Technical Reviewer

Steve Kurth is a digital graphic arts consultant, author, and trainer based in Portland, Maine. He is also the author of the *Adobe Illustrator 10 Shop Manual* and the upcoming *Hidden Secrets of Illustrator Web Graphics*, and co-author of *Digital Prepress Complete*. He has also been a technical editor for several other industry books. During the course of his work, Steve has developed and delivered customized training and solutions for an array of corporate clients including Verizon and LL Bean. He is a freelance cartoonist and illustrator who provided art for *Illustrator 9 and 10 for Dummies*. Steve is an Adobe Certified Expert in Photoshop, Acrobat PageMaker, and Illustrator.

Acknowledgments

Special thanks to the entire Photoshop team for continuing to improve an amazing product.

—Michael Ninness

Tell Us What You Think

As the reader of this book, you are the most important critic and commentator. We value your opinion and want to know what we're doing right, what we could do better, what areas you'd like to see us publish in, and any other words of wisdom you're willing to pass our way.

As Executive Editor for New Riders Publishing, I welcome your comments. You can fax, email, or write me directly to let me know what you did or didn't like about this book—as well as what we can do to make our books stronger. When you write, please be sure to include this book's title, ISBN, and author, as well as your name and phone or fax number. I will carefully review your comments and share them with the author and editors who worked on the book.

Please note that I cannot help you with technical problems related to the topic of this book, and that due to the high volume of email I receive, I might not be able to reply to every message.

Fax: 317-581-4663

Email: steve.weiss@newriders.com

Mail: Steve Weiss
            Executive Editor
            New Riders Publishing
            201 West 103rd Street
            Indianapolis, IN 46290 USA

Foreword

Rev Up in Adobe Photoshop with Fuel-Efficient Key Commands!

Tell me: Did you actually read the owner's manual after you bought your most recent new car? Hmmm? So, do you know how to open all the windows at the same time—simply by pressing those two little buttons? Can you activate the automatic tint on your windshield to reduce glare or increase brightness and contrast? And hey, how about that super-nifty hands-free auto-pilot feature that controls ALL the functions of your car?

Let me guess: You didn't even know these things were possible, and you're thinking, "Why didn't I read the manual?" Well, if you had read the manual, you would know that I'm totally out of my mind and that none of these automotive shortcuts really exist.

Now you're probably asking yourself, "What does this have to do with that great software, Adobe Photoshop and Adobe ImageReady?" (The answer to this question, by the way, is an astonishing revelation that only a few can comprehend.) But the point is, IF these amazing things were possible with your car, then Michael Ninness would know them. But, unfortunately, since his driver's license was revoked, Michael's had to focus his talents elsewhere. And so, combining his interest in Adobe Photoshop with his long days spent at the county courthouse, Michael has mastered every Adobe Photoshop and Adobe ImageReady shortcut known to man and mechanic and put them together in this one convenient book, *Photoshop 7 Power Shortcuts*.

I can personally say that *Photoshop 7 Power Shortcuts* presents every Adobe Photoshop and Adobe ImageReady shortcut in the known universe. So, at this moment in time, this book literally has it all. And if you're the type who wants to get where you're going fast in your car—whoops! I mean fast with Adobe Photoshop—this unique book is the single reference you should have within close reach when you're working in Adobe Photoshop.

I produce many tips and techniques for using Adobe software, and I know this book will come in handy for me. With its easy-to-use compendium of shortcuts, *Photoshop 7 Power Shortcuts* is a great resource to have right at your fingertips. I'm already finding that I can't live without it.

As I always say: "Good design! Good design! Good design!" You can never fail if you create something that's designed well! *Photoshop 7 Power Shortcuts* takes a simple idea, packages it in a good design, and—BINGO!—it's a winner!

I know I'll never double-click Adobe Photoshop again without it.

Russell Preston Brown
Senior Creative Director and Photoshop Evangelist
Adobe Systems Incorporated

Introduction

How many of you use Photoshop so much that you think of it as an operating system?

I got the idea for this book from all the sessions I have done over the years at various Photoshop conferences, classes, and seminars. Invariably, after I'm finished with a session, I am flooded by people coming up to me at the stage asking, "Now what was that keyboard shortcut you showed us again?"

As you will see in this book, more than 600 keyboard shortcuts are in Photoshop! A large number of them cannot be found in the manual that comes with Photoshop, nor are they listed in Photoshop's menus. This book lists them all, and more importantly, indexes them in an accessible way. Chances are there is a shortcut, or several, that you could be using—instead of doing things the way you do them today—that could literally save you minutes, even hours, a day.

And don't forget, if you can't remember what that one keyboard shortcut is, just hold down the entire left side of your keyboard and see what happens. Just don't EVER press (Macintosh: Cmd-Option-Shift-R) [Windows: Ctrl+Alt+Shift+R]! That reformats your hard drive.

How to Use This Book

There are several ways to use this book, but you will probably find that it is most useful when you want to see whether a shortcut is available for a particular tool or operation that you use a lot. Simply look in the index for that tool or command to find the page where the shortcut is listed. The shortcuts for both Macintosh and Windows versions of Photoshop will be listed.

Because several major releases of Photoshop exist, I've marked which versions (and which applications, because this book covers ImageReady) each shortcut will apply to. A solid box indicates the shortcut will work, and an empty box means it will not.

The 15 Tips You Must Learn. Quicker.

Your ultimate goal when mastering the Photoshop user interface is to make it as transparent as possible. When you want to switch to a different tool, change a brush size, or open a dialog box, you shouldn't have to stop what you're doing to waste your time looking for the tool, palette, menu item, and so on, choosing it, and then coming back to where you were. The true Photoshop gods simply press a key or key combination, and things just happen.

Hundreds of keyboard shortcuts are listed in this book. Don't try to memorize all of them all at once—you'll freak and get overwhelmed. Start by looking at the following Top 15 Tips list. Some of the items in the list are not single shortcuts, but are a category of shortcuts that you should commit to memory. Master one category, work them into your workflow, and then move on to the next category. After a while, something magical happens: The Photoshop UI becomes a subconscious thing, and you experience Pixel Nirvana. You think *Paintbrush tool*, and your finger instinctively presses the B key without you having to actually think the B key or even look at the keyboard.

This list is presented in the order that I recommend people memorize them, but of course, your mind probably works differently from mine, so do what works for you.

1. **Tool Shortcuts**

    Every tool has a letter assigned to it. To select the particular tool you want, just press its letter on the keyboard. Most of the shortcuts make sense, like M for the Marquee tool, E for the Eraser tool, and so on. Some tools on the toolbar actually house several options. To cycle through a tool slot's options, simply use Shift plus the letter for the tool. Starting in version 6.0, you can set a preference not to require the Shift key to cycle through a tool slot's tools (Edit > Preferences > General). The real power behind learning these particular shortcuts first is that when you know them all, it doesn't matter whether the Toolbar is actually open because you will be able to get to the tool you want at any time. See page 29–31 for a key to all the tools and their respective shortcuts.

2. **Brush Size**

Changing your brush size on the fly without moving your
mouse from the area that you are currently using the brush
on is a huge timesaver and keeps your brain centered on the
task at hand. Less than (<) and greater than (>) symbols
select the first and last brush. Left bracket ([) and right
bracket (]) decrease and increase the current brush size.
Shift-[and Shift-] decrease and increase the hardness of the
current brush. Comma (,) and period (.) select the next and
previous brush, but only if the current "working" brush did
not have its size or hardness changed with the shortcut keys.

3. **Move Tool**

The Move tool is arguably the most-used tool in Photoshop.
To that end, Adobe has made it easy to temporarily switch
to that tool when you are in any other tool. Just hold down
the (Cmd) [Ctrl] key while using any other tool.

Cmd/Ctrl gets to the Path Component Select Tool when
any Shape tool is selected.

Cmd/Ctrl gets to the Direct Selection Tool when any Pen
tool is selected.

This is the equivalent to switching to the Move tool for
Shapes and Paths.

4. **Palette Shortcuts**

Just like the tools, every palette has a keystroke assigned to
it to make showing and hiding palettes quick and efficient.
Learn them. Until you have them memorized, just keep
pressing any of the F5 through the F9 keys (F5 through F11
for ImageReady 2.0) until you see the palette tab you are
looking for. After a while, you will have them memorized,
and you won't think about it anymore.

Also, don't waste a lot of time opening and closing and
moving palettes around the screen. I arrange them on the
screen once and then leave them open at all times, always
keeping them in the same position. That way, I always know
where to look when I need to interact with a specific
palette, and they don't get lost behind each other. If they
get in the way, I just press the Tab key to hide them, and
then Tab again to bring them back.

New to Photoshop 7 is the ability to save the current palette configuration as a workspace preset. This makes it handy to save different palette scenarios and switch between them quickly. To save the current palette configuration as a new workspace, simply go to the Window > Workspaces > Save Workspace menu command and give it a useful name.

5. **Navigation Shortcuts**

Panning and zooming around an image can be a huge waste of time. Learn how to do it efficiently, and then raise your rates or ask for a raise. See pages 51–55 for all the navigation shortcuts. You'll notice that there are a lot of them. Pick one or two at a time to add to your repertoire, memorize them, and then add a couple more. After a while, you will begin to appreciate the subtle differences between them and, more importantly, when to use one instead of another.

6. **Contextual Menus**

The typical Photoshop user often overlooks this particular category of shortcuts, which is too bad because there is a contextual menu for just about everything in Photoshop. All the tools and most of the palettes have contextual menus that provide quick access to options and commands specific to that tool or palette. One of my favorites is the contextual menu for a Type layer that gives me a quick pop-up menu from which I can rasterize the type by choosing Render Layer. To access a contextual menu, hold down the Ctrl key on the Mac or the right-mouse button on Windows. See page 6 for a key to all the available contextual menus.

7. **Exchange Foreground and Background Colors**; reset Foreground and Background to Default Black and White

X for exchange, D for default. Next.

8. **Fill Commands**

Okay, it's time to face the fact that the Bucket tool is for wimps! Learn the Fill command shortcuts to quickly change the color of a selection or a layer. See pages 74–76 for all the Fill command shortcuts.

9. Layer Shortcuts

There are far too many shortcuts for creating, selecting, viewing, and moving layers to list here. The more of these you know, the more of a pro you will be. See pages 91–110.

10. Merging Layers

After you master creating, selecting, viewing, and moving layers, you will want to know the quick ways to merge and delete them, particularly the shortcuts for deleting multiple layers at once. See pages 107–108.

11. Opacity Shortcuts

Type a single number; the opacity changes to a 10% increment. Type two numbers quickly; the opacity changes to a 1% increment. For example, if you press 6, you get 60%. If you press 66 quickly, you get 66%. Just don't type 666—that reformats your hard drive. If you have the Move tool selected, you will be changing the opacity of the active layer. If you have a painting tool selected, you are changing the opacity of that tool. Otherwise, you will be changing the opacity of the active layer.

12. Multiple Undo/Redo Shortcuts

Learn these. Quicker. See page 23.

13. Revert

F12. Learn it, live it, love it.

14. Image→Adjust Dialog Shortcuts

Levels, Curves, Color Balance, and Hue/Saturation. You are in these dialog boxes every day! They all have shortcuts to open, reopen, and cancel them. Turn to pages 81–89 for these everyday dialog box shortcuts.

15. Reset Dialog Boxes

When you make a mistake while editing the values in a dialog box and you just want to start over from the beginning, don't bother clicking the Cancel button to reopen the dialog box. Just hold down the (Option) [Alt] key, and the Cancel button changes to a Reset button. The dialog will be reset to the same values it had when you first made it appear.

Palettes

Working Efficiently with Palettes

7.0   6.0   5.5   IR7   IR3
■   ■   ■   ■   ■

You know you are living large when you are working in Photoshop with dual monitors—one for the document window and one for all the palettes. For those of us who don't have two monitors, my general strategy for arranging the palettes is to group them in such a way that I can access any and all of the palettes using the default Function key assignments. In other words, not every palette has a Function key assigned to it, but as long as a given palette is grouped with a palette that does have a Function key assigned, you can get to that palette without having to pull down the menu.

When I watch people working in Photoshop, two of the most inefficient habits I see include constantly moving palettes all over the screen, and overlapping the palettes so that sometimes a palette gets hidden behind another palette. In Photoshop 6 and earlier versions, I overcame this by arranging the palettes on the screen one time, and then always left them in the same position. I just left them open all the time. If they were in the way, I simply pressed the Tab key to hide the palettes and got them out of the way.

Photoshop 7 speeds things up with its ability to store palette locations as custom workspaces. By arranging palettes as needed for a particular task and choosing Window→Workspace, you can create and access palette layouts tailored to the way you work. For example, you might want to create a workspace for image retouching where just the Brushes, History, and Color palettes are visible, and then create another for layout work that emphasizes the Layers palette. When you switch among tasks, you can switch among workspaces using the Window menu. To update a saved workspace, just save a new workspace with the same name and tell Photoshop to replace the existing workspace.

Contextual Menus

Mac: Ctrl + click

Win: Right-click

Don't forget about what perhaps is the single biggest timesaving feature of them all: contextual menus. Contextual menus provide you with literally hundreds of additional shortcuts. Too many people forget to incorporate this feature into their workflow.

I think my favorite contextual menu shortcut is using the Rasterize Layer command from the contextual menu: (Ctrl + click) [Right + click] on a Type layer. To find those that work best for you, just (Ctrl + click) [Right + click] on palettes and the canvas with various tools and note the options that appear. For example, depending on where in the Layers palette you click a styled vector, you can adjust its blending options, rasterize its mask, or adjust its layer effects.

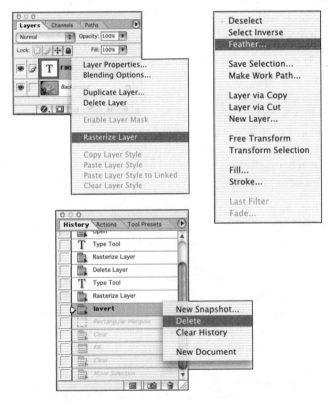

Show or Hide All Palettes

7.0 6.0 5.5 IR7 IR3
■   ■   ■   ■   ■

    Both: Tab

Show or Hide All but the Tool Palette

7.0 6.0 5.5 IR7 IR3
■   ■   ■   ■   ■

    Both: Shift + Tab

In Photoshop 6, Shift + Tab hides all but the Tool palette and the Options Bar.

Remove the Focus of a Numeric Edit Field in a Palette

7.0 6.0 5.5 IR7 IR3
■   ■   ■   ■   ■

    Both: Enter, Return, or Esc

Show or Hide the Navigator Palette

7.0 6.0 5.5 IR7 IR3
■   ■   ■   □   □

    Menu: Window→Showing/Hiding Navigator

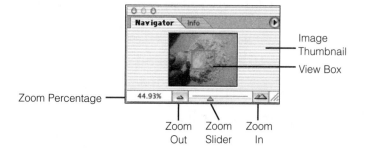

Image Thumbnail

View Box

Zoom Percentage

Zoom Out   Zoom Slider   Zoom In

Palettes

Show or Hide the Optimize Palette

7.0   6.0   5.5   IR7   IR3

Menu: Window→Showing/Hiding Optimize

Both: F10

Show or Hide the Options Palette

7.0   6.0   5.5   IR7   IR3

Menu: Window→Showing/Hiding Options

Both: Enter or Return

Mouse: Double-click a tool

In Photoshop 6 and 7 and ImageReady 7, the Options palette has been replaced with the Options bar at the top of the screen.

Brush size
and shape

Blending
mode

Show or Hide the Character Palette

7.0   6.0   5.5   IR7   IR3

Menu: Window→Showing/Hiding Character

Mac: Ctrl + T (while editing with the Type tool)

Win: Ctrl + T (while editing with the Type tool)

Photoshop 6 introduced on-canvas editing of text. In other words, you do not have to create and edit your text in a modal dialog box anymore. In both Photoshop 6 and ImageReady 3, there is no longer a Type palette. The options that were in the Type palette now appear in the Options bar when the Type tool is selected.

Show or Hide the Paragraph Palette

Menu: Window→Showing/Hiding Character

Mac: Ctrl + M (while editing with the Type tool)

Win: Ctrl + M (while editing with the Type tool)

Additionally, there are two new palettes for formatting text—the Character and Paragraph palettes.

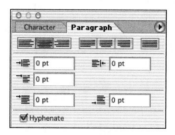

Show or Hide the Brushes Palette

7.0 6.0 5.5 IR7 IR3

Menu: Window→Showing/Hiding Brushes

Both: F5

This tip works in Photoshop 5.5 and 7.0, as well as ImageReady 2 and 7. In Photoshop 6 and ImageReady 3, the Brushes palette was replaced by the Options bar. When you select a painting tool, the Options bar will display the Brush options for the selected painting tool. Photoshop 7 and ImageReady 7 reintroduced the Brushes palette along with its old shortcut, F5.

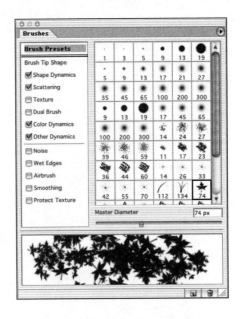

Show or Hide the Layers Palette

7.0 6.0 5.5 IR7 IR3

■ ■ ■ ■ ■

Menu: Window→Showing/Hiding Layers

Both: F7

Photoshop 7.0

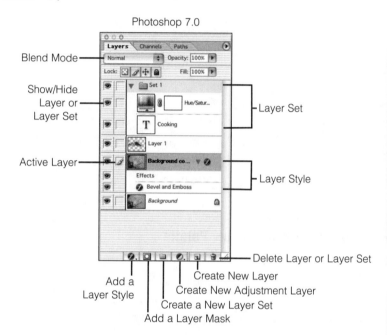

Blend Mode

Show/Hide Layer or Layer Set

Active Layer

Layer Set

Layer Style

Add a Layer Style

Create New Layer

Create New Adjustment Layer

Create a New Layer Set

Add a Layer Mask

Delete Layer or Layer Set

ImageReady 7

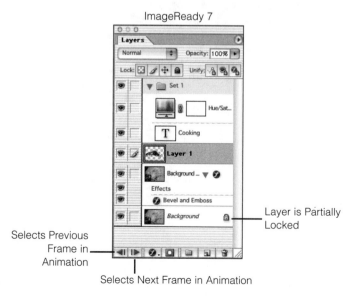

Layer is Partially Locked

Selects Previous Frame in Animation

Selects Next Frame in Animation

Palettes

Show or Hide the Layer Options/Effects Palette

7.0 6.0 5.5 IR7 IR3

Menu: Window→Showing/Hiding Layer Options/Effects

Show or Hide the Styles Palette

7.0 6.0 5.5 IR7 IR3

Menu: Window→Showing/Hiding Styles

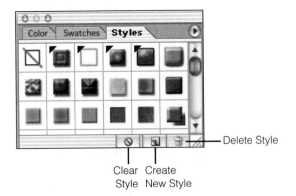

Show or Hide the Channels Palette

7.0 6.0 5.5 IR7 IR3
■ ■ ■ □ □

Menu: Window→Showing/Hiding Channels

Both: F7

F7 shows or hides the Layers palette. Also use it to show or hide the Channels palette if you haven't changed the default grouping of the Layers and Channels palettes. To show Channels if the Layers palette is not open, press F7, and then click the Channels tab. To hide both the Channels and the Layers palettes, press the F7 key until they both disappear.

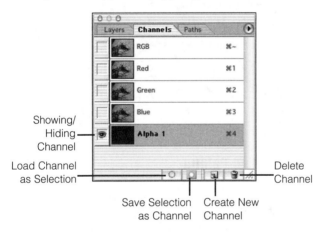

Showing/
Hiding
Channel

Load Channel
as Selection

Save Selection
as Channel

Create New
Channel

Delete
Channel

Show or Hide the Paths Palette

7.0 6.0 5.5 IR7 IR3
■ ■ ■ □ □

Menu: Window→Showing/Hiding Paths

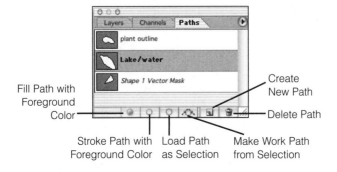

Fill Path with
Foreground
Color

Stroke Path with
Foreground Color

Load Path
as Selection

Make Work Path
from Selection

Create
New Path

Delete Path

Show or Hide the Actions Palette

7.0 6.0 5.5 IR7 IR3

■ ■ ■ ■ ■

Menu: Window→Showing/Hiding Actions

Both: F9

The only differences between the Photoshop and ImageReady Actions palette is that Photoshop allows for sets of actions whereas ImageReady does not, and ImageReady does not have a button mode for the palette.

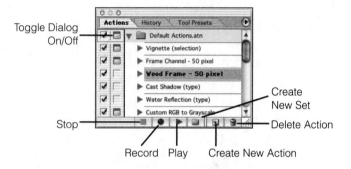

Toggle Dialog On/Off

Stop

Record Play   Create New Action

Create New Set

Delete Action

Show or Hide the Slice Palette

7.0 6.0 5.5 IR7 IR3

□ □ □ ■ ■

Menu: Window→Showing/Hiding Slice

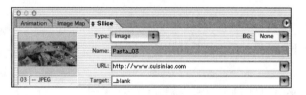

The Info Palette

Show or Hide the Info Palette

7.0 6.0 5.5 IR7 IR3
■   ■   ■   ■   ■

Menu: Window→Showing/Hiding Info

Both: F8

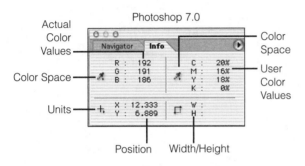

Actual Color Values — Photoshop 7.0 — Color Space — User Color Values — Color Space — Units — Position — Width/Height

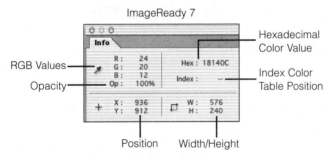

ImageReady 7 — Hexadecimal Color Value — RGB Values — Index Color Table Position — Opacity — Position — Width/Height

Change the Unit of Measure in the Info Palette

7.0 6.0 5.5 IR7 IR3
■   ■   ■   □   □

Mouse: Click on cross-hair icon pop-up

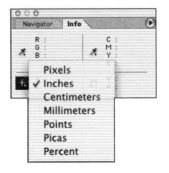

Pixels
✓ Inches
Centimeters
Millimeters
Points
Picas
Percent

Change the Color Mode of Readout

7.0 6.0 5.5 IR7 IR3

Mouse: Click on eyedropper icon pop-up

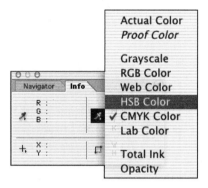

The Color Palette

Show or Hide the Color Palette

7.0 6.0 5.5 IR7 IR3

Menu: Window→Showing/Hiding Color

Both: F6

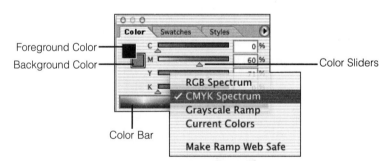

Foreground Color
Background Color
Color Sliders
Color Bar

Palettes

Set Background Color in the Color Palette

7.0 6.0 5.5 IR7 IR3
■ ■ ■ ■ ■

Mac: Option + click on color ramp

Win: Alt + click on color ramp

Cycle Through Color Ramps in the Color Palette

7.0 6.0 5.5 IR7 IR3
■ ■ ■ ■ ■

Mouse: Shift + click on color bar

The default color bar at the bottom of the Color palette displays the RGB color spectrum for quick selection of colors without having to open the Color Picker dialog box. You can change the ramp to display an RGB, CMYK, Grayscale, or Current Colors color.

Note: This only changes the color ramp, not the actual color slider controls in the palette that allow you to make precise value choices.

Choose a Specific Color Bar

7.0 6.0 5.5 IR7 IR3
■ ■ ■ ■ ■

Mac: Ctrl + click on color bar

Win: Right + click on color bar

This displays a contextual menu of the four different display choices for the color bar, plus the option to choose Make Ramp Web Safe.

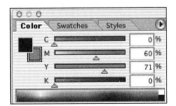

The Swatches Palette

Show or Hide the Swatches Palette

Menu: Window→Showing/Hiding Swatches

Both: F6

F6 shows or hides the Color palette. Also use it to show or hide the Swatches palette if you haven't changed the default grouping of the Color and Swatches palettes. To show Swatches if the Color palette is not open, press F6, and then click the Swatches tab. To hide both the Swatches and the Color palettes, press the F6 key until they both disappear.

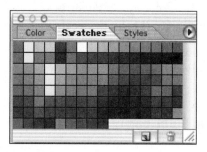

Choose a Swatch for the Foreground Color

Mouse: Click on a swatch

Choose a Swatch for the Background Color

7.0 6.0 5.5 IR7 IR3

Mac: Option + click on a swatch

Win: Alt + click on a swatch

In Photoshop 7.0 and ImageReady 7, Option/Alt-clicking a swatch deletes that swatch.

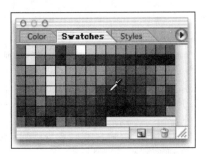

Add Foreground Color as a New Swatch

7.0 6.0 5.5 IR7 IR3

Mouse: Click on an empty slot in the Swatches palette

Look for the cursor to change into a bucket icon. In ImageReady, the only way to do this is to click on the New Swatch icon on the Swatches palette. You can also drag the current foreground and background colors from the Tools palette to the Swatches palette.

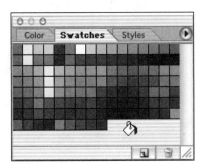

Palettes

Delete a Swatch

7.0 6.0 5.5 IR7 IR3

☐ ■ ■ ☐ ☐

Mac: Cmd + click a swatch

Win: Ctrl + click a swatch

In Photoshop 7.0 and ImageReady 3, option–/Alt-clicking a swatch deletes that swatch.

Look for the cursor to change into a scissors icon.

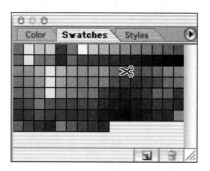

Insert Foreground Color as a New Swatch

7.0 6.0 5.5 IR7 IR3

☐ ■ ■ ☐ ☐

Mac: Option + Shift + click in the palette

Win: Alt + Shift + click in the palette

This inserts a swatch of the current foreground color and shifts the rest of the swatches in the palette to the right.

Replace a Swatch with the Foreground Color

7.0 6.0 5.5 IR7 IR3

■ ■ ■ ■ ■

Mouse: Shift + click a swatch

The Color Table

Show or Hide the Color Table

7.0 6.0 5.5 IR7 IR3

Menu: Window→Showing/Hiding Color Table

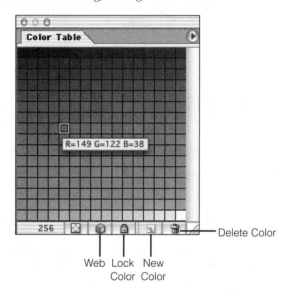

Web Lock New   Delete Color
     Color Color

Select Multiple Contiguous Colors in the Color Table Palette

7.0 6.0 5.5 IR7 IR3

Mouse: Shift + click a second color

Click the first color to select it. Shift + clicking a second color selects all the colors between the two colors. The second color you click becomes the current foreground color.

Select Multiple Discontiguous Colors in the Color Table Palette

7.0 6.0 5.5 IR7 IR3

Mac: Cmd + click a swatch

Win: Ctrl + click a swatch

The last color you click becomes the current foreground color.

Add Current Background Color to the Color Table

7.0   6.0   5.5   IR7   IR3
■   ■   ■   ■   ■

Mac: Option + click the New Color button

Win: Alt + click the New Color button

The History Palette

Show or Hide the History Palette

7.0   6.0   5.5   IR7   IR3
■   ■   ■   ■   ■

Menu: Window→Showing/Hiding History

Both: F9

F9 shows or hides the Actions palette. Also use it to show or hide the History palette if you haven't changed the default grouping of the Actions and History palette. To show History if the Actions palette is not open, press F9, and then click the History tab. To hide both the History and the Actions palettes, press the F9 key until they both disappear.

Photoshop Histories allow for snapshots whereas ImageReady does not. The Photoshop History palette has icons to create a new state and to create a new document from the current state; you won't find either of these in ImageReady.

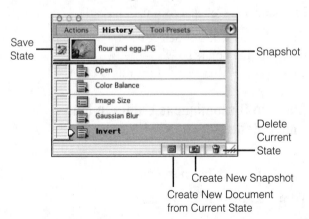

Save State — flour and egg..JPG — Snapshot

Open

Color Balance

Image Size

Gaussian Blur

Invert

Delete Current State

Create New Snapshot
Create New Document from Current State

Step Backward/Forward

Menu: History→Step Forward

Mac: Shift + Cmd + Z

Win: Shift + Ctrl + Z

Menu: History→Step Backward

Mac: Cmd + Option + Z

Win: Ctrl + Alt + Z

Photoshop 6 and ImageReady 3 allow you to choose from three different Redo shortcuts via the General Preferences. You can switch the Redo keystroke to match ImageReady, match Microsoft style, or remain Photoshop style. Note: Picking anything other than Photoshop style loses the ability to undo and redo history. The default in Photoshop 6 is that (Cmd + Z) [Ctrl + Z] toggles between undo and redo of the last thing you did. The default in ImageReady for (Cmd + Z) [Ctrl + Z] is set to multiple undo.

Here is what happens when you change the preferences:

Redo Key Preference Setting	History State Backward	History State Forward	Toggle Undo/Redo
(Cmd + Z) [Ctrl + Z] (Toggles Undo/Redo)	(Cmd + Option + Z) [Ctrl + Alt + Z]	(Cmd + Shift + Z) [Ctrl + Shift + Z]	(Cmd + Z) [Ctrl + Z]
(Cmd + Shift + Z) [Ctrl + Shift + Z]	(Cmd + Z) [Ctrl + Z]	(Cmd + Shift + Z) [Ctrl + Shift + Z]	(Cmd + Option + Z) [Ctrl + Alt + Z]
(Cmd + Y) [Ctrl + Y]	(Cmd + Z) [Ctrl + Z]	(Cmd + Y) [Ctrl + Y]	(Cmd + Option + Z) [Ctrl + Alt + Z]

Duplicate the History State (Other Than Current)

Mac: Option + click the state

Win: Alt + click the state

Create a New Snapshot

7.0 6.0 5.5 IR7 IR3
■ ■ ■ ☐ ☐

Mouse: Click the New Snapshot icon

Create a New Document from the Target Snapshot

7.0 6.0 5.5 IR7 IR3
■ ■ ■ ☐ ☐

Mouse: Click the New Document from Current State icon

The Animation Palette

Show or Hide the Animation Palette

7.0 6.0 5.5 IR7 IR3
■ ■ ■ ■ ■

Menu: Window→Showing/Hiding Animation

Both: F11

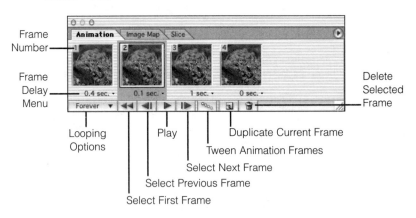

Frame Number

Frame Delay Menu

Looping Options

Play

Select First Frame

Select Previous Frame

Select Next Frame

Tween Animation Frames

Duplicate Current Frame

Delete Selected Frame

Create a New Frame in the Animation Palette

7.0 6.0 5.5 IR7 IR3
☐ ☐ ☐ ■ ■

Mac: Cmd + Option + Shift + F

Win: Ctrl + Alt + Shift + F

Go to First Frame

7.0 6.0 5.5 IR7 IR3
□   □   □   ■   ■

Mac: Option + Shift + left arrow

Win: Alt + Shift + left arrow

If the move tool is active when these frame navigation commands are selected, ImageReady will duplicate and move the selected layer.

Go to Last Frame

7.0 6.0 5.5 IR7 IR3
□   □   □   ■   ■

Mac: Option + Shift + right arrow

Win: Alt + Shift + right arrow

Go to Next Frame

7.0 6.0 5.5 IR7 IR3
□   □   □   ■   ■

Mac: Option + right arrow

Win: Alt + right arrow

Go to Previous Frame

7.0 6.0 5.5 IR7 IR3
□   □   □   ■   ■

Mac: Option + left arrow

Win: Alt + left arrow

Select Multiple Contiguous Frames

7.0 6.0 5.5 IR7 IR3
■   ■   ■   ■   ■

Mouse: Shift + click a frame

Select Multiple Discontiguous Frames

7.0 6.0 5.5 IR7 IR3
■   ■   ■   ■   ■

Mac: Cmd + click a frame

Win: Ctrl + click a frame

Palettes

Insert Pasted Frame After the Current Frame

7.0   6.0   5.5   IR7   IR3
☐   ☐   ☐   ■   ■

Both: Shift + Paste Frame

Normally, choosing Paste Frame from the Animation palette options menu adds the contents of the copied frame to the contents of the current frame. Holding down Shift inserts the copied contents into a new frame inserted after the current frame.

Duplicate the Layers Used in the Current Frame in the Layers Palette

7.0   6.0   5.5   IR7   IR3
☐   ☐   ☐   ■   ■

Mac: Cmd + Paste Frame

Win: Ctrl + Paste Frame

Normally, choosing Paste Frame from the Animation palette options menu adds the contents of the copied frame to the contents of the current frame. Holding down (Cmd) [Ctrl] duplicates the layers used in the frame in the Layers palette. It also includes the duplicated layers in the current frame.

Duplicate the Layers Used in the Current Frame in the Layers Palette and Insert Pasted Frame After the Current Frame

7.0   6.0   5.5   IR7   IR3
☐   ☐   ☐   ■   ■

Mac: Cmd + Shift + Paste Frame

Win: Ctrl + Shift + Paste Frame

Normally, choosing Paste Frame from the Animation palette options menu adds the contents of the copied frame to the contents of the current frame. Holding down (Cmd + Shift) [Ctrl + Shift] duplicates the layers used in the frame in the Layers palette. Also, rather than including the duplicated layers in the current frame, it inserts the copied contents into a new frame inserted after the current frame.

Replace the Destination Frame with the Copied Frame(s)

7.0	6.0	5.5	IR7	IR3
☐	☐	☐	■	■

Mac: Option + Shift + Paste Frame

Win: Alt + Shift + Paste Frame

Normally, choosing Paste Frame from the Animation palette options menu adds the contents of the copied frame to the contents of the current frame. Holding down the (Option + Shift) [Alt + Shift] keys replaces the contents of the destination frame with the contents of the copied frame(s).

Cancel Animation Play

7.0	6.0	5.5	IR7	IR3
■	■	■	■	■

Mac: Cmd + . (period)

Win: Ctrl + . (period)

Play or Stop Animation

7.0	6.0	5.5	IR7	IR3
■	■	■	■	■

Both: Shift + Spacebar

Move the Contents of the Selected Layer Concurrently in All Selected Animation Frames

7.0	6.0	5.5	IR7	IR3
■	■	■	■	■

Mac: Cmd + Shift + drag with the Move tool

Win: Ctrl + Shift + drag with the Move tool

Palettes

Tools

The Toolbar

In Photoshop 7, the Magnetic Pen tool is no longer a tool—it is an option for the Freeform Pen tool. Also in Photoshop 7, the Airbrush tool is no longer a tool—it is an option for any of the painting tools.

In addition, the default preference is set to require the Shift key to cycle through tool groups so that Photoshop 6 or 7 work as 5.0 and 5.5 did. You can set your preferences not to require the Shift key in the General Preferences dialog box.

Tools	Icon	PS 7	PS 6	PS 5.5	IR 7	IR 3
Rectangular Marquee		M	M	M	M	M
Elliptical Marquee		M	M	M	M	M
Cycle Marquee Tools		Shift + M	Shift + M	Shift + M	Shift + M	Shift + M
Move		V	V	V	V	V
Lasso		L	L	L	L	L
Polygonal Lasso		L	L	L	L	L
Magnetic Lasso		L	L	L	L	L
Cycle Lasso Tools		Shift + L	Shift + L	Shift + L	Shift + L	Shift + L
Magic Wand		W	W	W	W	W
Crop		C	C	C	C	C
Slice		K	K		K	K
Slice Select		K	K		K	K
Cycle Slice Tools		Shift + K	Shift + K		Shift K	Shift K
Airbrush			J	J	J	J
Paintbrush		B	B	B	B	B
Pencil		B	B	N	N	N
Cycle Brush, Pencil Tools		Shift + B	Shift + B			
Healing Brush		J				
Patch Tool		J				
Cycle Healing Brush, Patch Tools		Shift + J				
Cycle Pencil, Line tools				Shift + N		
Clone Stamp		S	S	S	S	S
Pattern Stamp		S	S	S		
Cycle Stamp Tools		Shift + S	Shift + S	Shift + S		
History Brush		Y	Y	Y		
Art History Brush		Y	Y	Y		
Cycle History Brush Tools		Shift + Y	Shift + Y	Shift + Y		

Tools	Icon	PS 7	PS 6	PS 5.5	IR 7	IR 3
Eraser		E	E	E	E	E
Magic Eraser		E	E	E	E	E
Background Eraser		E	E	E		
Cycle Eraser Tools		Shift + E	Shift + E	Shift + E	Shift + E	Shift + E
Gradient		G	G	G		
Cycle Gradient Tools				shift + G		
Bucket		G	G	K	G	G
Cycle Gradient, Bucket Tools		Shift + G	Shift + G			
Blur		R	R	R	R	R
Sharpen		R	R	R	R	R
Smudge		R	R	R	R	R
Cycle Blur, Sharpen, Smudge Tools		Shift + R	Shift + R	Shift + R	Shift + R	Shift + R
Dodge		O	O	O	O	O
Burn		O	O	O	O	O
Sponge		O	O	O	O	O
Cycle Dodge, Burn, Sponge Tools		Shift + O	Shift + O	Shift + O	Shift + O	Shift + O
Path Component Selection		A	A			
Direct Selection Tool		A	A	A		
Cycle Path Selection Tools		Shift + A	Shift + A			
Type		T	T	T	T	T
Type Mask				T		
Vertical Type				T		
Vertical Type Mask				T		
Cycle Type Tools				Shift + T		
Pen		P	P	P		
Freeform Pen		P	P	P		
Magnetic Pen				P		
Cycle Pen Tools		Shift + P	Shift + P	Shift + P		
Add Anchor Point		+	+	+		
Delete Anchor Point		-	-	-		

Tools	Icon	PS 7	PS 6	PS 5.5	IR 7	IR 3
Convert Anchor Point						
Rectangle Image Map					P	P
Circle Image Map					P	P
Polygon Image Map					P	P
Image Map Select					P	P
Cycle Image Map Tools					Shift + P	Shift + P
Rectangle		U	U		U	U
Rounded Rectangle					U	U
Ellipse		U	U		U	U
Polygon		U	U			
Line		U	U	N	U	U
Custom		U	U			
Cycle Shape Tools		Shift + U	Shift + U		Shift + U	Shift + U
Notes		N	N			
Audio Annotation		N	N			
Cycle Annotation Tools		Shift + N	Shift + N			
Eyedropper		I	I	I	I	I
Color Sampler Tool		I	I	I		
Measure		I	I	U		
Cycle Eyedropper Tools				Shift + 1		
Cycle Eyedropper, Measure Tools		Shift + I	Shift + I			
Hand		H	H	H	H	H
Zoom		Z	Z	Z	Z	Z
Default Colors		D	D	D	D	D
Exchange Colors		X	X	X	X	X
Toggle Quick Mask Mode		Q	Q	Q		
Cycle Screen Modes		F	F	F	F	F
Toggle Slice Visibility					Q	Q
Toggle Image Map Visibility					A	A
Rollover Preview					Y	Y

Tools

Cycle Through the Available Tools in a Tool Slot

7.0　6.0　5.5　IR7　IR3
■　■　■　■　■

Mac:　Option + click tool slot

Win:　Alt + click tool slot

If you want to use the mouse to switch from tool to tool rather than using the keystroke assigned to each tool, you can avoid using the tool slot fly-outs to switch to a tool that you can't see by (Option) [Alt] clicking on the tool slot. Keep clicking on the tool slot until the tool you want is selected.

Note: Not all tools are available in this manner—for example, the single-row or single-column selection tools. The only way to access these tools is to actually press on the Marquee tool slot and select them from the fly-out menu.

Toggle to the Move Tool

7.0　6.0　5.5　IR7　IR3
■　■　■　■　■

Mac:　Hold the Cmd key

Win:　Hold the Ctrl key

This allows you to temporarily switch to the Move tool while any other tool is selected (except the Path Selection, Pen, or Shape tools).

Toggle to Direct Select Tool

7.0　6.0　5.5　IR7　IR3
■　■　■　□　□

Mac:　Cmd

Win:　Ctrl

This allows you to temporarily switch to the Direct Select tool while the Path Selection or Shape tools are selected.

Tools

Toggle Between Polygonal Lasso and Lasso Tool

7.0 6.0 5.5 IR7 IR3

■   ■   ■   ■   ■

Mac: Option + drag or click

Win: Alt + drag or click

Holding down the modifier while in one of these two tools will toggle you to the other. If you are using the Polygonal Lasso tool, hold down the (Option) [Alt] key, and drag to switch to the Lasso tool behavior while the modifier key is held down. If you are using the Lasso too, hold down the (Option) [Alt] key, and click to switch to the Polygonal Lasso tool behavior while the modifier key is held down.

Specify the Clone Source for Clone (Rubber) Stamp Tool

7.0 6.0 5.5 IR7 IR3

■   ■   ■   ■   ■

Mac: Option + click

Win: Alt + click

Specify the Source Point for Healing Brush Tool

7.0 6.0 5.5 IR7 IR3

■   ■   ■   ■   ■

Mac: Option + click

Win: Alt + click

Tools

Rectangle Tool

7.0 6.0 5.5 IR7 IR3

■ □ □ ■ ■

Both: U

This tool is a shortcut in and of itself. It eliminates the need to create a new layer, use a selection tool to create a selected area, and then fill the area with color using a fill command by doing all of these steps for you. The Photoshop Rectangle tool can be used to add a pixel-based rectangle or to create paths and layer clipping paths. In ImageReady, the Rectangle tool is only for creating pixel rectangles.

Note: This shortcut actually takes you back to the last Shape tool you used, not necessarily the Rectangle tool.

Erase to History

7.0 6.0 5.5 IR7 IR3

■ ■ ■ □ □

Mac: Option + drag

Win: Alt + drag

Cycle Through Gradient List When the Gradient Tool Is Active

7.0 6.0 5.5 IR7 IR3

■ ■ □ □ □

Previous gradient   , (comma)
Next gradient   . (period)
First gradient   <
Last gradient   >

Cycle Through Gradient Types (Linear, Radial, etc.) When the Gradient Tool Is Active

7.0 6.0 5.5 IR7 IR3

■ ■ □ □ □

Previous gradient style   [
Next gradient style   ]

Toggle Between the Blur and Sharpen Tools

7.0 6.0 5.5 IR7 IR3
■   ■   ■   ■   ■

Mac: Option

Win: Alt

Holding down the modifier while in one of these two tools will toggle you to the other.

Smudge Using Foreground Color

7.0 6.0 5.5 IR7 IR3
■   ■   ■   □   □

Mac: Option

Win: Alt

This modify key toggles the finger painting mode for the Smudge tool. Finger painting starts by painting in a little bit of foreground color.

Toggle Between the Dodge and Burn Tools

7.0 6.0 5.5 IR7 IR3
■   ■   ■   ■   ■

Mac: Option

Win: Alt

Holding down the modifier while in one of these two tools will toggle you to the other.

Controlling the Toning Tools

7.0 6.0 5.5 IR7 IR3
□   □   ■   □   □

The Dodge, Burn, and Sponge tools can be modified to affect shadows, midtones, or highlights.

	Mac	Win
Shadows	Option + Shift + W	Alt + Shift + W
Midtones	Option + Shift + V	Alt + Shift + V
Highlights	Option + Shift + Z	Alt + Shift + Z

Tools

Controlling the Toning Tools

7.0 6.0 5.5 IR7 IR3

The Dodge, Burn, and Sponge tools can be modified to affect shadows, midtones, or highlights.

	Mac	Win
Shadows	Option + Shift + S	Alt + Shift + S
Midtones	Option + Shift + M	Alt + Shift + M
Highlights	Option + Shift + H	Alt + Shift + H

Set the Sponge Tool to Desaturate

7.0 6.0 5.5 IR7 IR3

Mac: Option + Shift + J

Win: Alt + Shift + J

Set the Sponge Tool to Desaturate

7.0 6.0 5.5 IR7 IR3

Mac: Option + Shift + D

Win: Alt + Shift + D

Set the Sponge Tool to Saturate

7.0 6.0 5.5 IR7 IR3

Mac: Option + Shift + A

Win: Alt + Shift + A

Set the Sponge Tool to Saturate

7.0 6.0 5.5 IR7 IR3

Mac: Option + Shift + S

Win: Alt + Shift + S

Tools

Toggle to the Direct Selection Tool

7.0   6.0   5.5   IR7   IR3
■   ■   ■   ☐   ☐

Mac: Cmd

Win: Ctrl

You can access the Direct Selection tool temporarily while you are in any of the Pen tools by holding down the (Cmd) [Ctrl] key.

Toggle to the Convert Direction Tool

7.0   6.0   5.5   IR7   IR3
■   ■   ■   ☐   ☐

Mac: Option

Win: Alt

Hold this key down while using the Pen tool to change the kind of point you will create when drawing a path.

Toggle to the Group Selection Function While Using the Direct Selection Tool

7.0   6.0   5.5   IR7   IR3
■   ■   ■   ☐   ☐

Mac: Option + click

Win: Alt + click

Note: The Group Selection is now the Path Selection tool in Photoshop 7.

Toggle the Text Mode Between Pixels and Mask

7.0   6.0   5.5   IR7   IR3
☐   ■   ☐   ☐   ☐

Both: [or {

Use the shortcut key right after you switch to the Type tool and before you start creating the text.

Photoshop 7 features separate tools for creating horizontal text, vertical text, and text masking. To cycle among them, use Shift + T.

Tools

Toggle the Text Orientation

7.0 6.0 5.5 IR7 IR3
☐ ■ ☐ ☐ ☐

Both:] or }

Use the shortcut key right after you switch to the Type tool and before you start creating the text.

Select Layer Style for Vector or Shape Tools

7.0 6.0 5.5 IR7 IR3
■ ■ ☐ ☐ ☐

Previous style	, (comma)
Next style	. (period)
First style	<
Last style	>

Note: This works only when the Shape tools are set to the option that creates a new shape layer.

Adjust Rounded Rectangle Tool Corner Radius

7.0 6.0 5.5 IR7 IR3
■ ■ ☐ ☐ ☐

Note: These shortcuts work only before you start drawing. They do not change the shape as you are drawing it or after you have drawn it.

Decrease by 1	[
Increase by 1	]
Decrease by 10	{
Increase by 10	}

Adjust Number of Sides for Polygon Tool

7.0 6.0 5.5 IR7 IR3
■ ■ ☐ ☐ ☐

Decrease by 1	[
Increase by 1	]
Decrease by 10	{
Increase by 10	}

Adjust Line Tool Weight

	7.0	6.0	5.5	IR7	IR3
	■	■	☐	☐	☐

Decrease by 1	[
Increase by 1	]
Decrease by 10	{
Increase by 10	}

Select Custom Shape

	7.0	6.0	5.5	IR7	IR3
	■	■	☐	☐	☐

Previous shape	[
Next shape	]
First shape	{
Last shape	}

Measure Constrained to a 45-Degree Axis

	7.0	6.0	5.5	IR7	IR3
	■	■	☐	☐	☐

Both: Shift + drag

The Measure tool must be selected for this to work.

Create a Protractor

	7.0	6.0	5.5	IR7	IR3
	■	■	■	☐	☐

Mac: Option + drag a measure endpoint

Win: Alt + drag an endpoint

This hidden feature allows you to create a second measurement line that you can use to measure angles. The Measure tool must be selected for this to work.

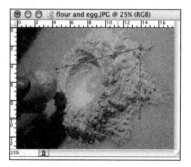

Tools

Changing the Canvas Color

7.0 6.0 5.5 IR7 IR3

Mouse: Shift + click on the canvas with the Bucket tool

To change the canvas color from the default gray to the current foreground color, hold down the Shift key and click the canvas with the Bucket tool. Mostly, this is a great practical joke to play on a coworker when he mistakenly leaves Photoshop open on his machine when he goes to lunch. Then you come in and change the canvas color to toxic green.

However, there is a practical reason to know about this shortcut: If you will be printing the image, it allows you to simulate what your image looks like against the color of the paper or background on which it will be printed.

Toggle to the Eyedropper Tool

7.0 6.0 5.5 IR7 IR3

Mac: Option

Win: Alt

Hold down the specified key to temporarily switch to the Eyedropper tool so that you can choose a new foreground color. This shortcut works when using any of the following tools: Airbrush, Paintbrush, Gradient, Paint Bucket, and Pencil.

Select Background Color When Using the Eyedropper Tool

7.0 6.0 5.5 IR7 IR3

Mac: Option + click

Win: Alt + click

Toggle to the Color Sampler Tool When Using the Eyedropper Tool

7.0 6.0 5.5 IR7 IR3

Both: Shift

You can Shift + click on the canvas to add a color sample point when a dialog box (like Levels, Curves, etc.) is open.

Tools

Delete a Color Sampler

7.0 6.0 5.5 IR7 IR3
■   ■   ■   □   □

Mac: Option + click

Win: Alt + click

Delete a Color Sampler

7.0 6.0 5.5 IR7 IR3
■   ■   ■   □   □

Mac: Option + Shift + click sampler

Win: Alt + Shift + click sampler

This works whenever you can see a color sampler.

Toggle to the Zoom Out Tool

7.0 6.0 5.5 IR7 IR3
■   ■   ■   ■   ■

Mac: Option + Spacebar

Win: Alt + Spacebar

Toggle to the Zoom In Tool

7.0 6.0 5.5 IR7 IR3
■   ■   ■   ■   ■

Mac: Cmd + Spacebar

Win: Ctrl + Spacebar

Zoom In

7.0 6.0 5.5 IR7 IR3
■   ■   ■   ■   ■

Menu: View→Zoom In

Mac: Cmd + + (plus)

Win: Ctrl + + (plus)

Mouse: Click with the Zoom (Magnifying Glass) tool

Tools

Zoom Out

Menu: View→Zoom Out

Mac: (Option + click) with the Zoom tool

Win: [Alt + click] with the Zoom tool

Mac: Cmd + – (minus)

Win: Ctrl + – (minus)

Zoom In Without Changing the Size of the Window

Mac: Cmd + Option + + (plus)

Win: Ctrl + Alt + + (plus)

Holding (Opt)/[Alt] reverses the behavior of the preference setting, "Keyboard Zoom Resizes Windows."

Zoom Out Without Changing the Size of the Window

Mac: Cmd + Option + – (minus)

Win: Ctrl + Alt + – (minus)

Invert the Quick Mask Selection Area

Mac: Option + click on the Quick Mask mode icon in the Tools palette

Win: Alt + click on the Quick Mask mode icon in the Tools palette

Tools

Open the Quick Mask Mode Dialog Box

7.0 6.0 5.5 IR7 IR3

Mouse: Double-click the Quick Mask mode icon in the Tools palette

> **Quick Mask Options**
>
> Color Indicates:
> ● Masked Areas
> ○ Selected Areas
>
> OK
> Cancel
>
> Color
> Opacity: 50 %

Toggle Menu Bar While in Full-Screen Mode

7.0 6.0 5.5 IR7 IR3

Both: Shift + F

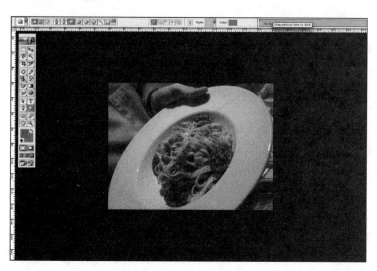

Set All Open Documents to the Same Screen Mode

7.0 6.0 5.5 IR7 IR3

Both: Shift + click on the desired screen mode icon in the Tools palette

Tools

Cropping Shortcuts

Apply Crop	7.0	6.0	5.5	IR7	IR3
	■	■	■	■	■

Both: Enter or Return

Cancel Crop	7.0	6.0	5.5	IR7	IR3
	■	■	■	■	■

Both: Esc

Mac: Cmd + . (period)

Win: Ctrl + . (period)

Crop Without Snapping to Edges	7.0	6.0	5.5	IR7	IR3
	■	■	■	■	■

Mac: Ctrl + drag

Win: Cmd + drag

Constrain Crop to a Square	7.0	6.0	5.5	IR7	IR3
	■	■	■	■	■

Mouse: Shift + drag corner handles

Resize Crop from the Center	7.0	6.0	5.5	IR7	IR3
	■	■	■	■	■

Mac: Option + drag handles

Win: Alt + drag handles

Constrain Crop from the Center	7.0	6.0	5.5	IR7	IR3
	■	■	■	■	■

Mac: Option + Shift + drag handles

Win: Alt + Shift + drag handles

Tools

Rotate the Cropping Boundary

7.0　6.0　5.5　IR7　IR3
■　■　■　■　■

Mouse: Drag outside the cropping box

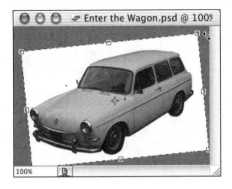

Move the Cropping Box

7.0　6.0　5.5　IR7　IR3
■　■　■　■　■

Mouse: Drag inside the cropping box

Tools

Resize the Cropping Box

7.0 6.0 5.5 IR7 IR3

Mouse: Drag cropping box handles

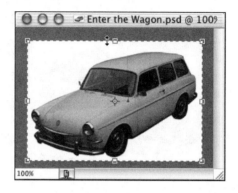

Add Canvas to an Image with the Crop Tool

7.0 6.0 5.5 IR7 IR3

Mouse: Resize cropping box beyond image area

This is another one of those cool hidden shortcuts because it isn't obvious at first. First, select the entire image area with the Crop tool. After you see the cropping box handles, you can then resize the box beyond the image area. When you apply the crop, it adds the additional canvas to the image area. To add canvas equally from the center of the image, hold down the (Option) [Alt] key while dragging a handle. Remember, you must create a crop area first, and then you can adjust it outside the image area. In ImageReady, you can crop beyond the canvas size directly—the Crop tool allows you to start drawing your crop rectangle outside of the canvas. To use this tip effectively, you should be in a Full Screen view mode.

Tools

Painting Shortcuts

Brush Selection Shortcuts

	7.0	6.0	5.5	IR7	IR3
	☐	☐	■	■	■

Mac and Win

Select the Next Brush	]
Select the Previous Brush	[
Select the First Brush	Shift + [
Select the Last Brush	Shift +]

Brush Selection Shortcuts

	7.0	6.0	5.5	IR7	IR3
	☐	■	☐	☐	☐

If the current brush was chosen from the brush presets in the Option bar, you can use the following shortcuts to select other brush presets:

Mac and Win

Next brush	. (period)
Previous brush	, (comma)
First brush	<
Last brush	>

Brush Editing Shortcuts

	7.0	6.0	5.5	IR7	IR3
	■	■	☐	☐	☐

Mac and Win

Enlarge brush diameter	]
Shrink brush diameter	[
Increase brush hardness	Shift +]
Decrease brush hardness	Shift + [

Tools

Create a New Brush

7.0 6.0 5.5 IR7 IR3
■ □ ■ □ □

Both: Click in empty slot

In Photoshop 6, you can also modify the current settings (diameter, angle, hardness, and spacing) of the currently selected brush. Photoshop 7 permits even more customization of properties, including texture, brush angle, and opacity jitter.

Delete a Brush

7.0 6.0 5.5 IR7 IR3
■ ■ ■ ■ ■

Mac: Opt + click the brush in the Brushes palette

Win: Alt + click the brush in the Brushes palette

Look for the cursor to change to a scissors icon.

Edit the Current Brush Preset

7.0 6.0 5.5 IR7 IR3
■ □ ■ ■ ■

Mouse: Double-click the brush

In Photoshop 7, double-clicking a brush preset allows you to rename the preset. Other modifications are made through the Brushes palette.

Decrease the Brush Radius

7.0 6.0 5.5 IR7 IR3
■ ■ □ □ □

Both: [

Increase the Brush Radius

7.0 6.0 5.5 IR7 IR3
■ ■ □ □ □

Both:]

Decrease the Brush Hardness

7.0 6.0 5.5 IR7 IR3
■ ■ □ □ □

Both: {

Tools

Increase the Brush Hardness

7.0 6.0 5.5 IR7 IR3

Both: }

Change Painting Tool Opacity in 1% Increments

7.0 6.0 5.5 IR7 IR3

Both: Type two numbers quickly (11=11%, 63=63%, and so on)

Change Painting Tool Opacity in 10% Increments

7.0 6.0 5.5 IR7 IR3

Both: Type a single number (1=10%, 2=20%, and so on)

Paint Constrained to Horizontal or Vertical Axis

7.0 6.0 5.5 IR7 IR3

Both: Shift + drag

This shortcut works when using any of the following tools:
Airbrush, Paintbrush, Rubber Stamp, Healing Brush, Pattern
Stamp, History Brush, Eraser, Pencil, Line, Blur, Sharpen, Smudge,
Dodge, Burn, Sponge, and Gradient.

Paint or Draw in a Straight Line

7.0 6.0 5.5 IR7 IR3

Mouse: Shift + click

This shortcut works when using any of the following tools:
Airbrush, Paintbrush, Rubber Stamp, Pattern Stamp, History
Brush, Eraser, Pencil, Pen, Line, Blur, Sharpen, Smudge, Dodge,
Burn, Sponge, and Gradient.

Tools

Set the Paint Bucket and Line Tools to Clear

7.0 6.0 5.5 IR7 IR3

■ ■ ■ □ □

Mac: Option + Shift + R

Win: Alt + Shift + R

Mouse: Blend Mode pop-up menu in Layers palette

Blend Mode Shortcuts

7.0 6.0 5.5 IR7 IR3

■ ■ ■ □ □

These shortcuts work only if you have a selection or the Move tool is the active tool. Otherwise, these shortcuts change the opacity of the active Painting tool. Blend modes can also be selected from the pop-up menu in the Layers palette.

Blend Mode	Mac	Win
Next Mode	Shift + + (plus)	
Previous Mode	Shift + – (minus)	
Normal (Threshold Mode in Bitmap documents)	Option + Shift + N	Alt + Shift + N
Dissolve	Option + Shift + I	Alt + Shift + I
Multiply	Option + Shift + M	Alt + Shift + M
Screen	Option + Shift + S	Alt + Shift + S
Overlay	Option + Shift + O	Alt + Shift + O
Soft Light	Option + Shift + F	Alt + Shift + F
Hard Light	Option + Shift + H	Alt + Shift + H
Linear Light	Option + Shift + V	Alt + Shift + V
Vivid Light	Option + Shift + J	Alt + Shift + J
Pin Light	Option + Shift + Z	Alt + Shift + Z
Color Dodge	Option + Shift + D	Alt + Shift + D
Color Burn	Option + Shift + B	Alt + Shift + B
Darken	Option + Shift + K	Alt + Shift + K
Lighten	Option + Shift + G	Alt + Shift + G
Difference	Option + Shift + E	Alt + Shift + E
Exclusion	Option + Shift + X	Alt + Shift + X
Hue	Option + Shift + U	Alt + Shift + U
Saturation	Option + Shift + T	Alt + Shift + T
Color	Option + Shift + C	Alt + Shift + C
Luminosity	Option + Shift + Y	Alt + Shift + Y
Behind	Option + Shift + Q	Alt + Shift + Q

Tools

Open Help

7.0 6.0 5.5 IR7 IR3
■ ■ ■ ■ ■

Menu: Help→Help Topics

Mac: Help key

Win: F1

Pan the Image

7.0 6.0 5.5 IR7 IR3
■ ■ ■ ■ ■

Both: Spacebar + drag

Mouse: Press and drag with the resulting Hand tool

To pan when using the Type tool, press (Cmd + Shift + Spacebar) [Ctrl + Shift + Spacebar] and drag with the resulting Hand tool.

Move View in Navigator Palette to New Area of Image

7.0 6.0 5.5 IR7 IR3
■ ■ ■ □ □

Both: Click in the preview area

Change View % and Keep Focus in the View % Edit Field of the Navigator Palette

7.0 6.0 5.5 IR7 IR3
■ ■ ■ □ □

Both: Shift + Return

If you have entered a number in the Zoom Percentage Field but are not sure if that's what you really want, press Shift + Return. This will zoom the image in or out to that percentage but keep the field in the Navigator palette active for quick entry of a new number.

Create New View in Navigator Palette

7.0 6.0 5.5 IR7 IR3
■ ■ ■ □ □

Mac: Cmd + drag in the preview area

Win: Ctrl + drag in the preview area

Toggle to the Zoom In Tool

7.0 6.0 5.5 IR7 IR3
■   ■   ■   ■   ■

Mac: Cmd + Spacebar

Win: Ctrl + Spacebar

Toggle to the Zoom In Tool

7.0 6.0 5.5 IR7 IR3
■   ■   ■   ■   ■

Mac: Cmd

Win: Ctrl

This shortcut is available only when the Hand tool is the active tool—if you have clicked either on the Hand tool or typed "H".

Toggle to the Zoom Out Tool

7.0 6.0 5.5 IR7 IR3
■   ■   ■   ■   ■

Mac: Option + Spacebar

Win: Alt + Spacebar

Toggle to the Zoom Out Tool

7.0 6.0 5.5 IR7 IR3
■   ■   ■   ■   ■

Mac: Option

Win: Alt

This shortcut is available only when the Hand tool is the active tool—if you have clicked either on the Hand tool or typed "H".

Zoom In

7.0 6.0 5.5 IR7 IR3
■   ■   ■   ■   ■

Menu: View→Zoom In

Mac: Cmd + + (plus)

Win: Shift + + (plus)

Mouse: Click with the Zoom tool

You can also click and drag to define the area to enlarge, and it will fill the current window.

Zoom Out

7.0 6.0 5.5 IR7 IR3
■   ■   ■   ■   ■

Menu: View→Zoom Out

Both: (Option + click) with the Zoom tool; [Alt + click] with the Zoom tool

Mac: Cmd + – (minus)

Win: Shift + – (minus)

Zoom to 100%

7.0 6.0 5.5 IR7 IR3
■   ■   ■   ■   ■

Menu: View→Fit on Screen

Mac: Cmd + Option + 0

Win: Shift + Alt + 0

Mouse: Double-click Zoom tool

Zoom to Fit On Screen

7.0 6.0 5.5 IR7 IR3
■   ■   ■   ■   ■

Menu: View→Actual Pixels

Mac: Cmd + 0

Win: Shift + 0

Mouse: Double-click Hand tool

This shortcut enlarges the window to fill as much space as the palettes leave it. Bonus tip: If you want to use the whole screen and don't mind if the image falls behind the palettes, hide the palettes by pressing the Tab key before using this shortcut.

Zoom In Without Changing the Window Size

7.0 6.0 5.5 IR7 IR3
■   ■   ■   ■   ■

Mac: Cmd + Option + + (plus)

Win: Shift + Alt + + (plus)

Holding (Opt)/[Alt] reverses the behavior of the preference setting "Keyboard Zoom Resizes Windows."

Zoom Out Without Changing the Window Size 7.0 6.0 5.5 IR7 IR3

■ ■ ■ ■ ■

Mac: Cmd + Option + – (minus)

Win: Shift + Alt + – (minus)

Holding (Opt)/[Alt] reverses the behavior of the preference
setting "Keyboard Zoom Resizes Windows."

Scroll Viewable Area of Image in Navigator Palette

7.0 6.0 5.5 IR7 IR3

■ ■ ■ ☐ ☐

Both: Drag view proxy

Scrolling Shortcuts 7.0 6.0 5.5 IR7 IR3

■ ■ ■ ■ ■

Scrolling one full screen left and right is available only in
Photoshop.

Distance	Mac	Win
Up One Full Screen	Page Up	Page Up
Down One Full Screen	Page Down	Page Down
Up 10 Pixels	Shift + Page Up	Shift + Page Up
Down 10 Pixels	Shift + Page Down	Shift + Page Down
Left One Full Screen	Cmd + Page Up	Ctrl + Page Up
Right One Full Screen	Cmd + Page Down	Ctrl + Page Down
Right 10 Pixels	Cmd + Shift + Page Down	Ctrl + Shift + Page Down
Left 10 Pixels	Cmd + Shift + Page Up	Ctrl + Shift + Page Up

Scroll to Upper-Left Corner of Image Window   7.0 6.0 5.5 IR7 IR3

■   ■   ■   ■   ■

Both: Home key

Power Tip: Spotting

When you want to remove dust and spots from an image, these keyboard shortcuts come in handy. Zoom up to the view you want to be in, usually 100%, and then press the Home key to begin in the upper-left corner of the image window. Then use the appropriate shortcuts to scroll down one screen at a time until you get to the bottom. After you get to the bottom, use the appropriate shortcut to scroll over one screen to the right, and then start scrolling up one screen at a time. Repeat this process until you end up in the lower-right corner of the image window. The advantage of using this method is that you are guaranteed not to miss any pixels in the image. Look at the Navigator palette to see where you are in the image.

Scroll to Lower-Right Corner of Image Window

7.0 6.0 5.5 IR7 IR3

■   ■   ■   ■   ■

Both: End key

Dialog Boxes

Editing Numeric Entry Values

7.0 6.0 5.5 IR7 IR3

■ ■ ■ ■ ■

These shortcuts work with most dialog boxes and sometimes edit the values by .1 rather than 1. This is true if the values allow decimal increments (for example, Feather) or by 1 rather than 10.

	Mac and Win
Increase Values by 1	Up Arrow
Increase Values by 10	Shift + Up Arrow
Decrease Values by 1	Down Arrow
Decrease Values by 10	Shift + Down Arrow

Cancel a Pop-Up Slider

7.0 6.0 5.5 IR7 IR3

■ ■ ■ ■ ■

Both: Esc

Mouse: Click outside the slider

Apply an Edit to a Pop-Up Slider

7.0 6.0 5.5 IR7 IR3

■ ■ ■ ■ ■

Both: Return or Enter

Cancel Any Dialog Box

7.0 6.0 5.5 IR7 IR3

■ ■ ■ ■ ■

Both: Esc

Mac: Cmd + . (period)

Win: Ctrl + . (period)

Activate Any Button in an Alert Dialog Box

7.0 6.0 5.5 IR7 IR3

■ ■ ■ ■ ■

Both: Type the first letter of the button (for example, D = Don't Save)

Dialog Boxes

Reset All Settings in a Dialog Box Without Exiting

7.0 6.0 5.5 IR7 IR3

Mac: Hold down Option to change the Cancel button to a Reset button

Win: Hold down Alt to change the Cancel button to a Reset button

Most of the Image > Adjustments dialogs support this, but some of the Filter dialogs do not.

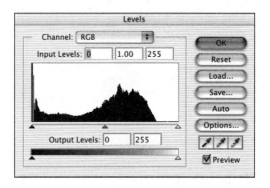

Pan Image While in a Dialog Box

7.0 6.0 5.5 IR7 IR3

Both: Spacebar + drag

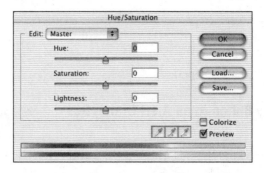

Zoom In While in a Dialog Box

7.0 6.0 5.5 IR7 IR3

Mac: Cmd + click or drag or Cmd + + (plus)

Win: Ctrl + click or drag or Ctrl + + (plus)

Many dialogs support this, but not all.

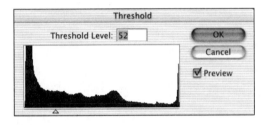

Zoom Out While in a Dialog Box

7.0 6.0 5.5 IR7 IR3

Mac: Option + click or drag or Cmd + – (minus)

Win: Alt + click or drag or Ctrl + – (minus)

The File Menu

File Commands

New

7.0	6.0	5.5	IR7	IR3
■	■	■	■	■

Menu: File→New

Mac: Cmd + N

Win: Ctrl + N

New with Last-Used Settings

7.0	6.0	5.5	IR7	IR3
■	■	■	■	■

Mac: Cmd + Option + N

Win: Ctrl + Alt + N

Sometimes you might notice that when you create a new document, it seems as if Photoshop is just making up numbers for the dimensions (and randomly choosing the mode as well). Don't worry, there is nothing random going on here. Photoshop automatically enters the attributes of any selection you may have copied to the Clipboard. (This is a cool timesaver in and of itself.) Use this shortcut if you want to bypass this behavior and force Photoshop to use the values of the last document you actually created.

Steal the Attributes of an Open Document

7.0	6.0	5.5	IR7	IR3
■	■	■	□	□

Menu: Window→Choose the document from the list. (In Photoshop 7, open documents are listed under the Window→Documents submenu.)

Here is another one of those deeply buried, not obvious, and undocumented shortcuts that makes you say, "Doh! I wish I knew that years ago!" When you are compositing images, it is often useful to make the canvas sizes of all the documents you are using the same. The three different places you can take advantage of this trick are the New dialog box, the Image Size dialog box, and the Canvas Size dialog box. When in any of these three places, you may have never noticed that most of the menus are grayed out and unavailable. However, the Window menu is available. If you choose any open document listed in the Window menu, Photoshop automatically changes the attributes of the New, Image Size, and Canvas Size dialog boxes to match the open document.

Open

7.0	6.0	5.5	IR7	IR3
■	■	■	■	■

Menu: File→Open

Mac: Cmd + O

Win: Ctrl + O

Open As

7.0	6.0	5.5	IR7	IR3
■	■	■	□	□

Win: Ctrl + Alt + O

Find

7.0	6.0	5.5	IR7	IR3
□	■	■	□	□

Both: Click the Find button in the Open dialog box

Mac: Cmd + F

Win: Ctrl + F

Can't find the image you are looking for? Don't remember what folder it is in? Don't sweat it. Make Photoshop do the work for you. Click the Find button or use the shortcut, type in the name or partial name of the file you are looking for, and have Photoshop find it. Photoshop displays the first occurrence of the name it finds for you. If that is not the correct file, use the Find Again command (Cmd + G) [Ctrl + G] until you find the file you are looking for. Note: You might not want to use this shortcut if you are hooked up to a network because it can get extremely slow.

Note: This shortcut can conflict with third-party utilities that launch their own find commands and is not available in the Photoshop 7 File Browser.

The File Menu

Browse

Menu: File→Open

Mac: Cmd + Shift + O

Win: Ctrl + Shift + O

The Browse command opens Photoshop 7's new File Browser. It's generally easiest to keep the File Browser docked to the Palette Well for quick access, but if you prefer to reserve that space for other palettes, this shortcut will come in handy. If you undock the File Browser and would like to re-dock it, use the command Dock to Palette Well in the File Browser's flyout menu.

File Browser

	Mac	Win
Open item	Double-click	Double-click
Navigation in the "folder navigation" view		
Up a folder	Up Arrow	Up Arrow
Down one folder	Down Arrow	Down Arrow
Up one level	Cmd + Up Arrow	Ctrl + Up Arrow
Down one level	Cmd + Down Arrow	Ctrl + Down Arrow
Expand all		"*" on keypad
Collapse all		"-" on keypad
Move to next pane		F6
Navigation in the "content area" view		
Move up one row	Up Arrow	Up Arrow
Move down one row	Down Arrow	Down Arrow
Move left one item	Left Arrow	Left Arrow
Move right one item	Right Arrow	Right Arrow
Go to first item	Home	Home
Go to last item	End	End
Scroll up one page	Page Up	Page Up
Scroll down one page	Page Down	Page Down
Rename item	Double-click name	Double-click name
Rename item	Enter	F2

...continues

The File Menu

The File Menu

	Mac	Win
Select all	Cmd + A	Ctrl + A
Add to selection	Shift + click or	Shift + click or
	Shift + Right/Left arrow	Shift + Right/Left arrow
Add to selection (discontiguous)	Cmd + click	Ctrl + click
Deselect all	Cmd + D	Ctrl + D
Rotate counterclockwise	Opt + click button	Alt + click button
Delete file or folder	Delete	Delete

Close

7.0 6.0 5.5 IR7 IR3
■   ■   ■   ■   ■

Menu: File→Close

Mac: Cmd + W

Win: Ctrl + W

Close All Documents

7.0 6.0 5.5 IR7 IR3
■   ■   ■   ■   ■

Menu: File→Close All

Mac: Cmd + Shift + W

Win: Ctrl + Shift + W

Save

7.0 6.0 5.5 IR7 IR3
■   ■   ■   ■   ■

Menu: File→Save

Mac: Cmd + S

Win: Ctrl + S

Save As

7.0 6.0 5.5 IR7 IR3
■   ■   ■   ■   ■

Menu: File→Save As

Mac: Cmd + Shift + S

Win: Ctrl + Shift + S

Save a Copy

7.0 6.0 5.5 IR7 IR3

Menu: File→Save a Copy

Mac: Cmd + Option + S

Win: Ctrl + Alt + S

In Photoshop 6 and 7, click the As A Copy check box in the Save/Save As dialog.

Save for Web

7.0 6.0 5.5 IR7 IR3

Menu: File→Save for Web

Mac: Cmd + Option + Shift + S

Win: Ctrl + Alt + Shift + S

Save Optimized

7.0 6.0 5.5 IR7 IR3

Menu: File→Save Optimized

Mac: Cmd + Option + S

Win: Ctrl + Alt + S

Save Optimized As

7.0 6.0 5.5 IR7 IR3

Menu: File→Save Optimized As

Mac: Cmd + Option + Shift + S

Win: Ctrl + Alt + Shift + S

Revert

7.0 6.0 5.5 IR7 IR3

Menu: File→Revert

Both: F12

The File Menu

The File Menu

Page Setup

7.0	6.0	5.5	IR7	IR3
☐	■	■	☐	☐

Menu: File→Page Setup

Mac: Cmd + Shift + P

Win: Ctrl + Shift + P

Image Info

7.0	6.0	5.5	IR7	IR3
☐	☐	☐	■	■

Menu: File→Image Info

Mac: Cmd + Shift + K

Win: Ctrl + Shift + K

Print Options

7.0	6.0	5.5	IR7	IR3
☐	■	☐	☐	☐

Menu: File→Print Options

Mac: Cmd + Option + Shift + P

Win: Ctrl + Alt + Shift + P

Photoshop 7 consolidates Print Options into Print with Preview and reserves this shortcut for Print One Copy. Print with Preview now gets the standard Print shortcut of (Cmd + P) [Ctrl + P], making it easier to find useful print options which might otherwise go unnoticed. If you prefer to use (Cmd + P) [Ctrl + P], you can adjust the Print Keys preference in General Preferences.

Print

7.0	6.0	5.5	IR7	IR3
■	■	■	■	■

Menu: File→Print

Mac: Cmd + P

Win: Ctrl + P

Photoshop 7 changes the Print shortcut to (Cmd + Opt + P) [Ctrl + Alt + P].

Print Preview

	7.0	6.0	5.5	IR7	IR3
	☐	☐	■	☐	☐

Menu: File→Print Options

Mac: Cmd + Option + P

Win: Ctrl + Alt + P

Print with Preview

	7.0	6.0	5.5	IR7	IR3
	■	☐	☐	☐	☐

Menu: File→Print with Preview

Mac: Cmd + P

Win: Ctrl + P

Print One Copy

	7.0	6.0	5.5	IR7	IR3
	■	☐	☐	☐	☐

Menu: File→Print One Copy

Mac: Cmd + Option + Shift + P

Win: Ctrl + Alt + Shift + P

Preview in [Default Browser]

	7.0	6.0	5.5	IR7	IR3
	☐	☐	☐	■	■

Menu: File→Preview In→[Default Browser]

Mac: Cmd + Option + P

Win: Ctrl + Alt + P

Jump to Photoshop from ImageReady and Vice Versa

	7.0	6.0	5.5	IR7	IR3
	■	■	■	■	■

Menu: File→Jump To

Mac: Cmd + Shift + M

Win: Ctrl + Shift + M

The File Menu

Quit

7.0	6.0	5.5	IR7	IR3
■	■	■	■	■

Menu: File→Quit

Mac: Cmd + Q

Win: Ctrl + Q

Preferences

Preferences

7.0	6.0	5.5	IR7	IR3
☐	☐	■	☐	☐

Menu: File→Preferences

Mac: Cmd + K

Win: Ctrl + K

Note: Preferences appear under the Edit menu in Photoshop 6 and 7 and ImageReady 3 and 7. Please see "The Edit Menu" chapter for more information.

Switch Plug-Ins Folder or Scratch Disk When Launching Photoshop

7.0	6.0	5.5	IR7	IR3
■	■	☐	☐	☐

Mac: Hold down Cmd + Option when launching Photoshop

Win: Hold down Ctrl + Alt when launching Photoshop

Not many people know these two tricks. If you hold down these two keys when you launch Photoshop, you will reveal two secret dialog boxes. The first dialog box allows you to specify which Plug-ins folder you want to use for this Photoshop session. You can arrange your plug-ins into different folders and then only use a certain set. For instance, maybe you are going to use Photoshop for the next three hours to do color correction, and you don't need the 112 special effects plug-ins you have installed. Throw all your production plug-ins into a separate folder and then choose that folder on startup. This saves Photoshop from wasting RAM on plug-ins you don't need to use at that time. After you've located and selected the folder you want, hold down the modifier keys again and another dialog box appears.

The second dialog box allows you to choose which volume you want to use as the scratch disk. This is handy because if you know that you want to change it from the last time you used Photoshop, this allows you to make the change when you start up. If you didn't know about this shortcut, you'd have to open Photoshop, make the scratch disk change in the Preferences dialog box, and then quit and restart Photoshop for it to take effect.

Note: Photoshop 7 will not bring up the dialog box for selecting the Plug-ins folder on Mac or Windows. The dialog for the scratch disk comes up as described.

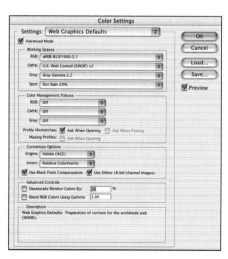

Open Color Settings Dialog Box

7.0 6.0 5.5 IR7 IR3

Menu: Edit→Color Settings

Mac: Cmd + Shift + K

Win: Ctrl + Shift + K

The File Menu

Toggle Precise Cursors

7.0   6.0   5.5   IR7   IR3

Menu: File→Preferences→Display & Cursors

Both: Caps Lock

Precise Cursors changes the display of the current tool into a cross-hair target. The Caps Lock key allows you to toggle this setting regardless of the Display & Cursors setting in the Preferences dialog box.

The File Menu

The Edit Menu

Edit Commands

Undo/Redo

		7.0	6.0	5.5	IR7	IR3
		■	■	■	□	□

Command	Menu	Mac	Win
Undo	Edit→Undo	Cmd + Z	Ctrl + Z
Redo	Edit→Redo	Cmd + Z	Ctrl + Z
Toggle Undo/ Redo Last Step	Edit→Undo/Redo	Cmd + Z	Ctrl + Z

Step Backward/Forward

		7.0	6.0	5.5	IR7	IR3
		■	■	□	■	■

Menu: History→Step Forward

Mac: Cmd + Shift + Cmd + Z

Win: Ctrl + Shift + Ctrl + Z

Menu: History→Step Backward

Mac: Cmd + Option + Z

Win: Ctrl + Alt + Z

Photoshop 6 and ImageReady 3 allow you to choose from three different Redo shortcuts via the General Preferences. You can switch the Redo keystroke to match ImageReady, match Microsoft style, or remain Photoshop style.

Note: Picking anything other than Photoshop style removes the ability to undo and redo history via the keyboard. If you decide to use an option other that Photoshop style, you can still use the History palette to perform multiple undo and redo.

The default in Photoshop 6 is that (Cmd + Z) [Ctrl + Z] toggles between undo and redo of the last thing you did. The default in ImageReady for (Cmd + Z) [Ctrl + Z] is set to multiple undo.

Here is what happens when you change the preferences:

Redo Key Preference setting	History State Backward	History State Forward	Toggle Undo/Redo
(Cmd + Z) [Ctrl + Z] (Toggles Undo/Redo)	(Cmd + Option+ Z) [Ctrl+ Alt + Z]	(Cmd + Shift+ Z) [Ctrl + Shift + Z]	(Cmd + Z) [Ctrl + Z]
(Cmd + Shift + Z) [Ctrl + Shift + Z]	(Cmd + Z) [Ctrl + Z]	(Cmd + Shift + Z) [Ctrl + Shift + Z]	(Cmd + Option + Z) [Ctrl + Alt + Z]
(Cmd + Y) [Ctrl + Y]	(Cmd + Z) [Ctrl + Z]	(Cmd + Y) [Ctrl + Y]	(Cmd + Option + Z) [Ctrl + Alt + Z]

Fade

7.0 6.0 5.5 IR7 IR3

■ ■ □ □ □

Menu: Edit→Fade name of the filter or command

Mac: Cmd + Shift + F

Win: Ctrl + Shift + F

This is a great shortcut to adjust the intensity of a particular effect, such as a brush stroke or filter, by playing with the opacity or the blend mode of the applied effect. "Fade" is something of a misnomer because the command can also add intensity (for example, raising the opacity a brush stroke applied at 35% to 70%). In Photoshop 5.5, you'll find the menu item under the Filter menu.

Cut

7.0 6.0 5.5 IR7 IR3

■ ■ ■ ■ ■

Menu: Edit→Cut

Mac: Cmd + X

Win: Ctrl + X

Copy

7.0 6.0 5.5 IR7 IR3
■   ■   ■   ■   ■

Menu: Edit→Copy

Mac: Cmd + C

Win: Ctrl + C

Copy Merged

7.0 6.0 5.5 IR7 IR3
■   ■   ■   ■   ■

Menu: Edit→Copy Merged

Mac: Cmd + Shift + C

Win: Ctrl + Shift + C

Paste

7.0 6.0 5.5 IR7 IR3
■   ■   ■   ■   ■

Menu: Edit→Paste

Mac: Cmd + V

Win: Ctrl + V

Paste Into

7.0 6.0 5.5 IR7 IR3
■   ■   ■   □   □

Menu: Edit→Paste Into

Mac: Cmd + Shift + V

Win: Ctrl + Shift + V

Copy HTML Code for Selected Slices

7.0 6.0 5.5 IR7 IR3
□   □   □   ■   ■

Menu: Edit→Copy HTML Code→Copy Selected Slices

Mac: Cmd + Option + C

Win: Ctrl + Alt + C

The Edit Menu

Fill Commands

Open the Fill Dialog Box

7.0   6.0   5.5   IR7   IR3
■   ■   ■   ■   ■

Menu: Edit→Fill

Mac: Shift + Delete

Win: Shift + Backspace

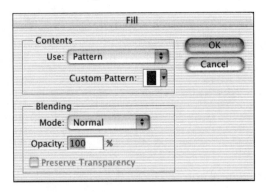

Fill with the Foreground Color

7.0   6.0   5.5   IR7   IR3
■   ■   ■   ■   ■

Menu: Edit→Fill

Mac: Option + Delete

Win: Alt + Backspace

Mouse: Bucket tool

This command fills the entire contents of the active layer or selection with the foreground color, unless the Preserve Transparency (Lock Transparent Pixels in Photoshop 6 and 7) check box is turned on in the Layers palette.

Fill with the Foreground Color While Preserving Transparency

7.0 6.0 5.5 IR7 IR3

Menu: Edit→Fill

Mac: Option + Shift + Delete

Win: Alt + Shift + Backspace

This command changes the color of the layer only where there are actual pixels. All transparent areas are unchanged. This is an extremely efficient way to change the color of text on a Type layer.

Note: Type layers always have Preserve Transparency (Lock Transparent Pixels check box in Photoshop 6 and 7) turned on, so you *can* use the regular fill shortcuts. However, I recommend you remember this shortcut instead because it still works. That way, you only have to remember one shortcut for changing the color of type, whether it is a Type layer, or a Type layer that has been rasterized.

Fill with the Background Color While Preserving Transparency

7.0 6.0 5.5 IR7 IR3

Menu: Edit→Fill

Mac: Cmd + Shift + Delete

Win: Ctrl + Shift + Backspace

This command changes the color of the layer only where there are actual pixels. All transparent areas are unchanged. This is an extremely efficient way to change the color of text on a Type layer.

Note: Type layers always have Preserve Transparency turned on, so you *can* use the regular fill shortcuts. However, I recommend you remember this shortcut instead because it still works. That way, you only have to remember one shortcut for changing the color of type, whether it is a Type layer, or a Type layer that has been rendered.

The Edit Menu

Fill with the Background Color

7.0   6.0   5.5   IR7   IR3

■ ■ ■ ■ ■

Menu: Edit→Fill

Mac: Cmd + Delete

Win: Ctrl + Backspace

This command fills the entire contents of the active layer or selection with the background color.

Fill from History

7.0   6.0   5.5   IR7   IR3

■ ■ ■ □ □

Menu: Edit→Fill

Mac: Cmd + Option + Delete

Win: Ctrl + Alt + Backspace

This command fills the entire contents of the active layer or selection with the active History state.

Transformations

Skew Using Center Point

7.0   6.0   5.5   IR7   IR3

■ ■ ■ ■ ■

Mac: Cmd + Option + drag a middle handle

Win: Ctrl + Alt + drag a middle handle

A middle handle means any of the non-corner handles.

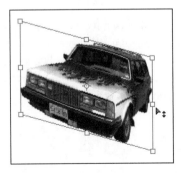

Scale Using Center Point

7.0	6.0	5.5	IR7	IR3
■	■	■	■	■

Mac: Option + drag a corner handle

Win: Alt + drag a corner handle

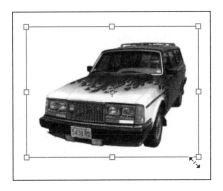

Snap Angle Values to 15-Degree Increments

7.0	6.0	5.5	IR7	IR3
■	■	■	■	■

Both: Shift + drag angle wheel

Apply Any Transformation

7.0	6.0	5.5	IR7	IR3
■	■	■	■	■

Both: Enter or Return

Cancel Any Transformation

7.0	6.0	5.5	IR7	IR3
■	■	■	■	■

Both: Esc

Mac: Cmd + . (period)

Win: Ctrl + . (period)

Free Transform

7.0	6.0	5.5	IR7	IR3
■	■	■	■	■

Menu: Edit→Free Transform

Mac: Cmd + T

Win: Ctrl + T

The Edit Menu

Transform Again

7.0 6.0 5.5 IR7 IR3
■   ■   ■   ■   ■

Menu: Edit→Transform→Again

Mac: Cmd + Shift + T

Win: Ctrl + Shift + T

This shortcut repeats the last transformation settings you used.

Create a Duplicate While Transforming

7.0 6.0 5.5 IR7 IR3
■   ■   ■   ■   ■

Mac: Cmd + Option + T

Win: Ctrl + Alt + T

Create a Duplicate While Transforming Again

7.0 6.0 5.5 IR7 IR3
■   ■   ■   ■   ■

Mac: Cmd + Option + Shift + T

Win: Ctrl + Alt + Shift + T

This shortcut creates a duplicate and repeats the last transformation settings you used.

Skew Using Center Point and Constrain the Axis

7.0 6.0 5.5 IR7 IR3
■   ■   ■   ■   ■

Mac: Cmd + Option + Shift + drag a middle handle

Win: Ctrl + Alt + Shift + drag a middle handle

A middle handle means any of the non-corner handles.

Create Perspective While Using Free Transform

7.0 6.0 5.5 IR7 IR3
■   ■   ■   ■   ■

Mac: Cmd + Option + Shift + drag a corner handle

Win: Ctrl + Alt + Shift + drag a corner handle

The Edit Menu

Distort Freely While Using Free Transform

7.0 6.0 5.5 IR7 IR3

■ ■ ■ ■ ■

Mac: Cmd + drag a handle

Win: Ctrl + drag a handle

Preferences

Preferences

7.0 6.0 5.5 IR7 IR3

☐ ☐ ■ ☐ ☐

Menu: File→Preferences

Mac: Cmd + K

Win: Ctrl + K

Note: Preferences are available on Mac OS X by choosing the application menu (Photoshop→Preferences). Apple had instituted new interface guidelines for OS X-native applications, some of which conflict with existing Photoshop shortcuts. To use the OS X-standard shortcuts, enable the preference Use System Shortcut Keys in General Preferences. Enabling the preference changes the following shortcuts:

	Enabled	Disabled
View→Show Extras	Cmd + Ctrl + H	Cmd + H
Image→Adjust→Curves	Cmd + Ctrl + M	Cmd + M
Window→Minimize	Cmd + M	Cmd + Ctrl + M
Hide Application	Cmd + H	Cmd + Ctrl + H

Accessing Other Preference Panels from the Photoshop General Preferences Panel

7.0 6.0 5.5 IR7 IR3

■ ■ ■ ☐ ☐

Panel	Mac	Win
General	Cmd + 1	Ctrl + 1
Saving Files	Cmd + 2	Ctrl + 2
Display & Cursors	Cmd + 3	Ctrl + 3
Transparency & Gamut	Cmd + 4	Ctrl + 4

...continues

The Edit Menu

Panel	Mac	Win
Units & Rulers	Cmd + 5	Ctrl + 5
Guides & Grid	Cmd + 6	Ctrl + 6
Plug-Ins & Scratch Disks	Cmd + 7	Ctrl + 7
Image Cache (Mac)	Cmd + 8	
Memory & Image Cache (Win)		Ctrl + 8
Next Panel	Cmd + N	Ctrl + N
Previous Panel	Cmd + P	Ctrl + P

In Photoshop 7, "Saving Files" has been renamed "File Handling."

Accessing Other Preference Panels from the ImageReady General Preferences Panel

7.0 6.0 5.5 IR7 IR3
☐ ☐ ☐ ■ ■

Panel	Mac	Win
General	Cmd + 1	Ctrl + 1
Slices	Cmd + 2	Ctrl + 2
Image Maps	Cmd + 3	Ctrl + 3
Optimization	Cmd + 4	Ctrl + 4
Cursors	Cmd + 5	Ctrl + 5
Transparency	Cmd + 6	Ctrl + 6
Plug-Ins & Scratch Disks	Cmd + 7	Ctrl + 7
Next Panel	Cmd + N	Ctrl + N
Previous Panel	Cmd + P	Ctrl + P

In Windows, "Plug-Ins & Scratch Disks" is named "Plug-Ins."

Reopen the Last Option Panel Used in Preferences

7.0 6.0 5.5 IR7 IR3
■ ■ ■ ■ ■

Menu: Edit→Preferences

Mac: Cmd + Option + K

Win: Ctrl + Alt + K

The Edit Menu

The Image Menu

Image Adjustment Commands

Color Balance

	7.0	6.0	5.5	IR7	IR3
	■	■	■	☐	☐

Menu: Image→Adjustments→Color Balance

Mac: Cmd + B

Win: Ctrl + B

Color Balance with Last-Used Settings

	7.0	6.0	5.5	IR7	IR3
	■	■	■	☐	☐

Mac: Cmd + Option + B

Win: Ctrl + Alt + B

Auto Contrast

	7.0	6.0	5.5	IR7	IR3
	■	■	■	■	■

Menu: Image→Adjustments→Auto Contrast

Mac: Cmd + Option + Shift + L

Win: Ctrl + Alt + Shift + L

Auto Color

7.0   6.0   5.5   IR7   IR3

■   □   □   □   □

Menu: Image→Adjustments→Auto Color

Mac: Cmd + Option + Shift + B

Win: Ctrl + Alt + Shift + B

Desaturate Image

7.0   6.0   5.5   IR7   IR3

■   ■   ■   ■   ■

Menu: Image→Adjustments→Desaturate

Mac: Cmd + Shift + U

Win: Ctrl + Shift + U

Invert

7.0   6.0   5.5   IR7   IR3

■   ■   ■   ■   ■

Menu: Image→Adjustments→Invert

Mac: Cmd + I

Win: Ctrl + I

See Original While in an Adjust Dialog Box

7.0   6.0   5.5   IR7   IR3

□   □   ■   □   □

Mouse: Press dialog box title bar with Preview off

This shortcut allows you to quickly compare the original image with the adjusted image, while still in any of the Image→Adjustments dialog boxes (Levels, Curves, Color Balance, Hue/Saturation, and so on). However, as you make adjustments in the dialog box, the entire monitor gets adjusted, not just the image window.

The Image Menu

In versions before Photoshop 6, this feature works only when you have Video LUT Animation turned on in your Display & Cursors Preferences, and when the Preview check box is turned off in the Levels dialog box. Also, an additional note for Windows users: This feature works only if your video card supports Video LUT Animation.

Levels Commands

Levels

7.0	6.0	5.5	IR7	IR3
■	■	■	■	■

Menu: Image→Adjustments→Levels

Mac: Cmd + L

Win: Ctrl + L

Levels with Last-Used Settings

7.0	6.0	5.5	IR7	IR3
■	■	■	□	□

Mac: Cmd + Option + L

Win: Ctrl + Alt + L

Auto Levels

7.0	6.0	5.5	IR7	IR3
■	■	■	■	■

Menu: Image→Adjustments→Auto Levels

Mac: Cmd + Shift + L

Win: Ctrl + Shift + L

The Image Menu

Show Clipping Using Video LUT

7.0   6.0   5.5   IR7   IR3

☐   ☐   ■   ☐   ☐

Mac: Option + drag sliders with Preview off

Win: Alt + drag sliders with Preview off

This shortcut shows you which areas in your image are blowing out to complete white or black as you make tonal adjustments to the highlights and shadows of your image. In versions before Photoshop 6, this feature works only when you have Video LUT Animation turned on in your Display & Cursors Preferences, and when the Preview check box is turned off in the Levels dialog box. Also, an additional note for Windows users: This feature works only if your video card supports Video LUT Animation.

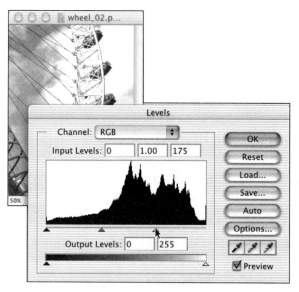

Curves Commands

Curves

7.0   6.0   5.5   IR7   IR3

■   ■   ■   ☐   ☐

Menu: Image→Adjustments→Curves

Mac: Cmd + M

Win: Ctrl + M

Curves with Last-Used Settings

7.0   6.0   5.5   IR7   IR3

■ ■ ■ □ □

Mac: Cmd + Option + M

Win: Ctrl + Alt + M

Pinpoint Color in Image and Place Point on Curve

7.0   6.0   5.5   IR7   IR3

■ ■ ■ □ □

Mac: Cmd + click in image

Win: Ctrl + click in image

If you click anywhere in an image window while the Curves dialog box is open, a hollow circle appears on the curve and shows you where the specific color directly under the cursor falls on the curve.

If you hold down the (Cmd) [Ctrl] key and then click in the image, a solid circle is added to the curve so that you can actually edit that specific range of color. This helps you use a visual approach to color correction. In Photoshop 7, this now also works in CMYK mode.

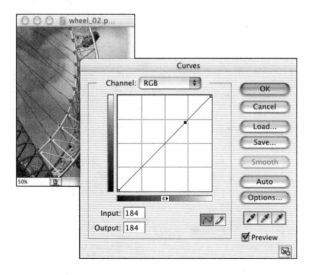

Pinpoint Color in Image and Place Points on Each Curve

7.0 6.0 5.5 IR7 IR3

Mac: Cmd + Shift + click in image

Win: Ctrl + Shift + click in image

If you click anywhere in an image window while the Curves dialog box is open, a hollow circle appears on the curve and shows you where the specific color directly under the cursor falls on the curve.

If you hold down the (Cmd + Shift) [Ctrl + Shift] keys and then click in the image, a solid circle is added to each of the individual channel's curves so that you can actually edit that specific range of color. This helps you use a visual approach to color correction.

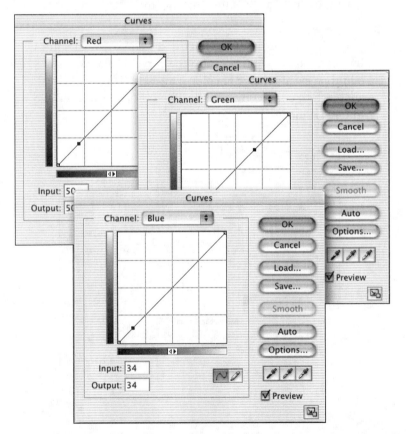

Select Next Control Point on Curve

7.0	6.0	5.5	IR7	IR3
☐	☐	■	☐	☐

Mac: Cmd + Tab

Win: Ctrl + Tab

Select Previous Control Point on Curve

7.0	6.0	5.5	IR7	IR3
☐	☐	■	☐	☐

Mac: Cmd + Shift + Tab

Win: Ctrl + Shift + Tab

Select Multiple Points

7.0	6.0	5.5	IR7	IR3
■	■	■	☐	☐

Both: Shift + click

Add Point to Curve

7.0	6.0	5.5	IR7	IR3
■	■	■	☐	☐

Both: Click in grid

Delete Point from Curve

7.0	6.0	5.5	IR7	IR3
■	■	■	☐	☐

Mac: Cmd + click point

Win: Ctrl + click point

Move Point(s)

7.0	6.0	5.5	IR7	IR3
■	■	■	☐	☐

Both: Arrow keys

Select a point or points first, and then you can move them with the arrow keys.

The Image Menu

Move Point(s) in Larger Increments Than One

7.0	6.0	5.5	IR7	IR3
■	■	■	☐	☐

Both: Shift + Arrow keys

Select a point or points first, and then you can move them with the arrow keys.

Deselect All Selected Points

7.0	6.0	5.5	IR7	IR3
☐	☐	■	☐	☐

Mac: Cmd + D

Win: Ctrl + D

Toggle the Size of the Grid in the Curves Dialog Box Between 10% and 25% Increments

7.0	6.0	5.5	IR7	IR3
■	■	■	☐	☐

Mac: Option + click on grid

Win: Alt + click on grid

Hue/Saturation Commands

Hue/Saturation

7.0	6.0	5.5	IR7	IR3
■	■	■	■	■

Menu: Image→Adjustments→Hue/Saturation

Mac: Cmd + U

Win: Ctrl + U

Hue/Saturation with Last-Used Settings

7.0	6.0	5.5	IR7	IR3
■	■	■	☐	☐

Mac: Cmd + Option + U

Win: Ctrl + Alt + U

The Image Menu

Move Range to a New Location

7.0 6.0 5.5 IR7 IR3
■   ■   ■   □   □

Mouse: Click in image

This works only when you're seeing the range—that is, not when you're using the Master option from the pop-up menu.

Add to Range

7.0 6.0 5.5 IR7 IR3
■   ■   ■   □   □

Mouse: Shift + click/drag in image

Subtract from Range

7.0 6.0 5.5 IR7 IR3
■   ■   ■   □   □

Mac: Option + click/drag in image

Win: Alt + click/drag in image

Edit Master

7.0 6.0 5.5 IR7 IR3
■   ■   ■   □   □

Mac: Cmd + ~ (tilde)

Win: Ctrl + ~ (tilde)

Edit Individual Colors

7.0 6.0 5.5 IR7 IR3
■   ■   ■   □   □

Mac: Cmd + (1–6)

Win: Ctrl + (1–6)

Color	Number
Reds	1
Yellows	2
Greens	3
Cyans	4
Blues	5
Magentas	6

Note: The Extract and Liquify commands have moved from the Image menu to the Filter menu in Photoshop 7. Please see the chapter, "The Filter Menu," for these shortcuts.

The Image Menu

Layers

Creating and Deleting Layers

Create a New Layer with the New Layer Dialog Box

7.0   6.0   5.5   IR7   IR3

Menu: Layer→New→Layer

Mac: Option + click New Layer icon or Cmd + Shift + N

Win: Alt + click New Layer icon or Ctrl + Shift + N

This method presents the New Layer dialog box, giving you a chance to name the new layer and specify other options such as Opacity and Blend Mode as you create the layer.

Layers

Create a New Layer and Bypass the New Layer Dialog Box

Menu: (Option) + Layer→New→Layer;
[Alt] + Layer→New→Layer

Mac: Cmd + Option + Shift + N

Win: Ctrl + Alt + Shift + N

Mouse: Click the New Layer icon

This shortcut skips the New Layer dialog box when creating a new layer. Layers are named automatically (Layer 1, Layer 2, and so on). Just hold down the specified modifier key as you choose the menu command.

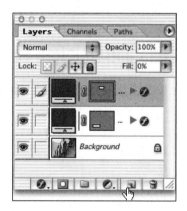

New Layer Via Copy

7.0 6.0 5.5 IR7 IR3

Menu: Layer→New→Layer Via Copy

Mac: Cmd + J

Win: Ctrl + J

This shortcut copies the current selection and places it on a new layer, as long as the selection is on an active and visible layer.

New Layer Via Cut

7.0 6.0 5.5 IR7 IR3
■   ■   ■   ■   ■

Menu: Layer→New→Layer Via Cut

Mac: Cmd + Shift + J

Win: Ctrl + Shift + J

This shortcut cuts the current selection from the current layer and places it on a new layer, as long as the selection is on an active and visible layer.

New Layer Via Copy with Make Layer Dialog Box

7.0 6.0 5.5 IR7 IR3
■   ■   ■   ■   ■

Menu: Layer→New→Layer Via Copy

Mac: Cmd + Option + J

Win: Ctrl + Alt + J

This shortcut copies the current selection and places it on a new layer. The Make Layer dialog also appears, giving you a chance to name the new layer and choose other options such as Group with Previous or choose a Layer Blending Mode.

Duplicate a Layer with the New Layer Dialog Box

7.0 6.0 5.5 IR7 IR3
■   ■   ■   □   □

Mac: Cmd + Option + J

Win: Ctrl + Alt + J

Mouse: (Option) [Alt] drag the layer to the New Layer button

This method presents the New Layer dialog box, giving you a chance to name the new layer and specify other options such as opacity and blend mode as you create the layer.

Note: This shortcut is not available in ImageReady.

New Layer Via Cut with Make Layer Dialog Box

7.0 6.0 5.5 IR7 IR3

■ ■ ■ ■ ■

Menu: Layer→New→Layer Via Cut

Mac: Cmd + Option + Shift + J

Win: Ctrl + Option + Shift + J

This shortcut cuts the current selection and places it on a new layer. The Make Layer dialog also appears, giving you a chance to name the new layer.

Create a New Layer Below the Active Layer

7.0 6.0 5.5 IR7 IR3

□ □ □ □ ■

Mac: Cmd + Shift + J

Win: Ctrl + Shift + J

Random. Only in ImageReady 3.0—stump your friends.

Duplicate a Layer, Part 1

7.0 6.0 5.5 IR7 IR3

■ ■ ■ ■ ■

Mac: Cmd + J

Win: Ctrl + J

Mouse: Drag the layer to the New Layer icon

This is normally the Layer via Copy command. It copies a selection into its own layer. However, when there is no active selection, this command duplicates the active layer instead. Thank you Mark and Marc!

Duplicate a Layer, Part 2

7.0 6.0 5.5 IR7 IR3

■ ■ ■ ■ ■

Mac: Cmd + Option + Arrow key

Win: Ctrl + Alt + Arrow key

Mouse: Drag the layer to the New Layer icon

Okay, this is kind of a lame shortcut, but because this book claims to have ALL of the shortcuts in it, I've got to include this one. This shortcut also moves the duplicated layer one pixel in the direction of the arrow key that you used. So if you plan on moving the duplicated layer anyway, this is no big deal and is a great short-cut. However, if you need the duplicated layer to be in the exact same position as the original, you will need to press the opposite arrow key once to get it back to the original position. Note that this shortcut does not work on the Background layer because the Background layer is always locked by default.

Note: If there is an active selection, this shortcut actually duplicates the selection and moves it on the target layer—not on a duplicate layer.

Create a New Adjustment Layer

7.0 6.0 5.5 IR7 IR3

☐ ☐ ■ ☐ ☐

Menu: Layer→New→Adjustment Layer

Mac: Cmd + click the New Layer icon

Win: Ctrl + click the New Layer icon

This shortcut is no longer necessary as of Photoshop 6, and doesn't even work in Photoshop 7, because the Layers palette now has a specific icon for creating Adjustment Layers.

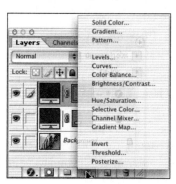

Delete a Layer

7.0 6.0 5.5 IR7 IR3

■ ■ ■ ■ ■

Mouse: Click the Delete Layer icon

Layers

Delete a Layer and Skip the Warning Alert   7.0 6.0 5.5 IR7 IR3

Mac: Option + click the Delete Layer icon

Win: Alt + click the Delete Layer icon

Delete Multiple Layers, Part 1   7.0 6.0 5.5 IR7 IR3

Both: Merge Visible, and then click the Delete Layer icon

There is no way to select multiple layers to delete them all at once. However, there is a shortcut. First, hide all the layers you want to keep, and then use the Merge Visible shortcut to merge all the layers you want to delete into a single layer. Now, simply delete this single composite layer.

Delete Multiple Layers, Part 2   7.0 6.0 5.5 IR7 IR3

Both: Use the Merge Linked command

In an odd twist, when you use the Merge or Merge Linked command with linked layers that are hidden, they get deleted! So, if there are several layers you want to get rid of, use the shortcut to hide all the layers but one, and then link all the layers you want to delete to the target layer. When you use the Merge or Merge Linked command, all the linked layers are deleted, although the visible target layer is kept.

In Photoshop 6 and 7, you have a new option. Link the layers you want to delete and (Cmd + click) [Ctrl + click] the Trash icon in the Layers palette. All the linked layers will be deleted. (Cmd + Option + click) [Ctrl + Alt + click] will delete the linked layers while bypassing the confirmation dialog. Use with caution: If any layer sets are linked, all the layers in the set will be deleted as well.

Showing and Selecting Layers

Show or Hide a Layer

7.0 6.0 5.5 IR7 IR3

■   ■   ■   ■   ■

Mouse: Click in Eye icon area

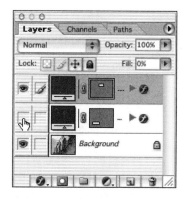

Show Just This Layer/Show All Layers

7.0 6.0 5.5 IR7 IR3

■   ■   ■   ■   ■

Mac: Option + click in Eye icon area

Win: Alt + click in Eye icon area

View and Select One Layer at a Time

7.0 6.0 5.5 IR7 IR3

■   ■   ■   ■   ■

Mac: Option + click layer name

Win: Alt + click layer name

This tip works when only one layer is currently visible. In other words, hide all other layers except one. Then you can use this tip to simultaneously show the next layer you select and hide the previously shown layer.

Note: There is a subtle difference here when clicking the layer name versus clicking the eyeball area. If you click the eyeball area instead, the previous layer stays selected as the active layer, not the layer you just clicked the eyeball for.

Layers

Show/Hide Multiple Layers

7.0 6.0 5.5 IR7 IR3

Mouse: Drag through Eye icon area

Activating Layers

7.0 6.0 5.5 IR7 IR3

	Mac	Win
Next Visible Layer (Up)	Option +]	Alt +]
Previous Visible Layer (Down)	Option + [	Alt + [
Bottom Layer	Option + Shift + [	Alt + Shift + [
Top Layer	Option + Shift +]	Alt + Shift +]

If only one layer is visible when you use this shortcut, then the next layer activates and becomes visible, and the previous layer gets hidden. This is a quick way to isolate and cycle through your layer stack by viewing one layer at a time by using this shortcut repeatedly.

Select a Layer by Name

7.0 6.0 5.5 IR7 IR3

Mac: Ctrl + click the canvas

Win: Right + click the canvas

This shortcut works only when the Move tool is active. If you currently have a different tool selected, you can add (Cmd) [Ctrl] to the shortcut to temporarily switch to the Move tool. This shortcut displays a pop-up menu that lists all the available layers directly under the cursor, as long as a layer actually has some pixels under the cursor. Simply choose the layer you want from the list. This shortcut illustrates the need for you to always name your layers something relevant rather than using the default names of Layer 1, Layer 2, and so on.

Select the Topmost Visible Layer

7.0 6.0 5.5 IR7 IR3
■   ■   ■   ■   ■

Mac: Cmd + Ctrl + Option + click

Win: Ctrl + Alt + Right + click

This shortcut selects the topmost layer directly under the cursor.

Editing Layers

Change Layer Opacity in 1% Increments

7.0 6.0 5.5 IR7 IR3
■   ■   ■   ■   ■

Both: Type two numbers quickly (11=11%, 63=63%, and so on)

This shortcut works only when you have an active selection or the Move tool is the active tool. Otherwise, this shortcut changes the opacity of the active Painting tool.

Change Layer Opacity in 10% Increments

7.0 6.0 5.5 IR7 IR3
■   ■   ■   ■   ■

Both: Type a single number (1=10%, 2=20%, and so on)

This shortcut works only when you have an active selection or the Move tool is the active tool. Otherwise, this shortcut changes the opacity of the active Painting tool.

Blend Mode Shortcuts

7.0 6.0 5.5 IR7 IR3
■   ■   ■   ■   ■

These shortcuts work only when the active tool doesn't support blend modes. Otherwise, this shortcut changes the opacity of the active painting tool. Blend modes can also be selected from the pop-up menu in the Layers palette.

Blend Mode	Mac	Win
Next Mode	Shift + + (plus)	
Previous Mode	Shift + - (minus)	
Normal / Threshold (bitmap mode only)	Option + Shift + N	Alt + Shift + N

...continues

Blend Mode	Mac	Win
Dissolve	Option + Shift + I	Alt + Shift + I
Multiply	Option + Shift + M	Alt + Shift + M
Screen	Option + Shift + S	Alt + Shift + S
Overlay	Option + Shift + O	Alt + Shift + O
Soft Light	Option + Shift + F	Alt + Shift + F
Hard Light	Option + Shift + H	Alt + Shift + H
Linear Light	Option + Shift + V	Alt + Shift + V
Vivid Light	Option + Shift + J	Alt + Shift + J
Pin Light	Option + Shift + Z	Alt + Shift + Z
Color Dodge	Option + Shift + D	Alt + Shift + D
Color Burn	Option + Shift + B	Alt + Shift + B
Darken	Option + Shift + K	Alt + Shift + K
Lighten	Option + Shift + G	Alt + Shift + G
Difference	Option + Shift + E	Alt + Shift + E
Exclusion	Option + Shift + X	Alt + Shift + X
Hue	Option + Shift + U	Alt + Shift + U
Saturation	Option + Shift + T	Alt + Shift + T
Color	Option + Shift + C	Alt + Shift + C
Luminosity	Option + Shift + Y	Alt + Shift + Y

Edit Layer Options

7.0 6.0 5.5 IR7 IR3

Menu: Layer→Layer Options

Mouse: Double-click layer thumbnail or layer name

By popular request, in Photoshop 7, Adobe has restored the ability to rename a layer simply by double-clicking the layer name. Layer properties remain accessible by double-clicking the layer thumbnail.

Edit Layer Properties

7.0 6.0 5.5 IR7 IR3

Menu: Layer→Layer Properties

Mac: Option + double-click layer thumbnail or layer name

Win: Alt + double-click layer thumbnail or layer name

Edit Blending Modes and Layer Styles

7.0 6.0 5.5 IR7 IR3

Menu: Layer→Layer Style

Mouse: Double-click layer thumbnail or layer name

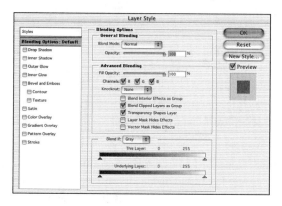

Edit Adjustment Layer Options

7.0 6.0 5.5 IR7 IR3

Menu: Layer→Adjustment Options

Mouse: Double-click Adjustment icon

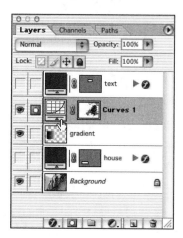

Layers

Convert the Background Layer

7.0 6.0 5.5 IR7 IR3
■ ■ ■ ■ □

Mouse: Double-click the background layer and change its name

Or, in versions prior to 6.0, with the Move tool selected, nudge the layer up and then down by one pixel, using the up and down arrow keys.

The Background layer cannot support transparency. Use these shortcuts to convert the Background layer into a layer that does support transparency. The default name is Layer 0, but you can change the name to anything you want. You also need to convert the Background layer if you want to reposition it in the layer stack.

Note: If you want to add a Background layer back to a file, the only choice is to use the Layer→New→Background menu command. (In Photoshop 6 and 7, the menu selection is Layer→New→Background from Layer. If a Background layer already exists, the menu selection is Layer→New→Layer from Background.)

Moving Layers

Move Layer One Pixel

7.0 6.0 5.5 IR7 IR3
■ ■ ■ ■ ■

Menu: Edit→Transform→Numeric

Both: Arrow keys

As long as the Move tool is active, the arrow keys move a layer one pixel in the direction of the arrow key you choose. If any other tool is active, hold down the (Cmd) [Ctrl] key, and then use the arrow keys.

Move Layer 10 Pixels

7.0 6.0 5.5 IR7 IR3
■   ■   ■   ■   ■

Menu: Edit→Transform→Numeric

Both: Shift + Arrow keys

As long as the Move tool is active, holding down the Shift key and then pressing the arrow keys moves a layer 10 pixels in the direction of the arrow key you choose. If any other tool is active, hold down the (Cmd + Shift) [Ctrl + Shift] keys, and then use the arrow keys.

Move Target Layer Up

7.0 6.0 5.5 IR7 IR3
■   ■   ■   ■   ■

Menu: Layer→Arrange→Bring Forward

Mac: Cmd +]

Win: Ctrl +]

Move Target Layer Down

7.0 6.0 5.5 IR7 IR3
■   ■   ■   ■   ■

Menu: Layer→Arrange→Send Backward

Mac: Cmd + [

Win: Ctrl + [

Move Target Layer to Top

7.0 6.0 5.5 IR7 IR3
■   ■   ■   ■   ■

Menu: Layer→Arrange→Bring to Front

Mac: Cmd + Shift +]

Win: Ctrl + Shift +]

Layers

Move Target Layer to Bottom

7.0 6.0 5.5 IR7 IR3

■ ■ ■ ■ ■

Menu: Layer→Arrange→Send to Back

Mac: Cmd + Shift + [

Win: Ctrl + Shift + [

Note: If the file has a Background layer, the target layer will stop above the Background layer. To move a layer below the Background layer, you must convert the Background layer to a layer that supports transparency first.

Center When Dragging from One File to Another

7.0 6.0 5.5 IR7 IR3

■ ■ ■ ■ ■

Mouse: Shift + drag from one document to the other

If you want the selection or layer from one document to end up in the middle of the document to which you are dragging it, hold down the Shift key and drag the item to the target document. Let go of the mouse before letting go of the Shift key.

Note: If the canvas sizes of the two documents are the same, holding down the Shift key places the dragged item in the target document in the same position as the original document.

Register Items When Dragging from One Document to Another

7.0 6.0 5.5 IR7 IR3

■ ■ ■ ■ ■

Mouse: Shift + drag from one document to the other

If you want the selection or layer from one document to end up in the same position in the target document to which you are dragging it, make sure that they both have the same canvas size. Hold down the Shift key as you drag the item to the target document. Let go of the mouse before letting go of the Shift key.

Note: If the canvas sizes of the two documents are different, holding down the Shift key places the dragged item in the center of the target document.

Linking and Grouping Layers

Link a Layer (or Layer Set) to Current Target Layer

7.0 6.0 5.5 IR7 IR3

■ ■ ■ ■ ■

Mouse: Click in the Link icon area

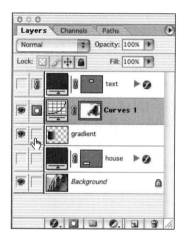

Turn On/Off Linking for Multiple Layers (or Layer Sets)

7.0 6.0 5.5 IR7 IR3

■ ■ ■ ■ ■

Mouse: Drag in the Link icon area

Link with the Topmost Visible Layer

7.0 6.0 5.5 IR7 IR3

■ ■ ■ □ □

Mac: Cmd + Ctrl + Shift + click

Win: Ctrl + Shift + right-click

This shortcut displays a pop-up menu that lists all the available layers directly under the cursor. Instead of selecting a layer, the layer you choose will be linked with the current active layer.

Link/Unlink Layers from the Layer Contextual Menu

7.0 6.0 5.5 IR7 IR3

Mac: Ctrl + Shift + click

Win: Shift + right-click

If you have the Move tool selected, (Ctrl + click) [right-click] in
the composition displays the contextual menu for selecting layers.
If you are in a tool other than the Move tool, (Cmd + Ctrl +
click) [Ctrl + right-click] temporarily switches you to the Move
tool.

Group Target Layer with Layer Below

7.0 6.0 5.5 IR7 IR3

Menu: Layer→Group with Previous

Mac: Cmd + G

Win: Ctrl + G

Ungroup Target Layer with Layer Below

7.0 6.0 5.5 IR7 IR3

Menu: Layer→Ungroup

Mac: Cmd + Shift +G

Win: Ctrl + Shift + G

Toggle Group/Ungroup with Previous Layer

7.0 6.0 5.5 IR7 IR3

Mac: Option + click divider between layers

Win: Alt + click divider between layers

Merging Layers

Merge Target Layer into the Layer Below

7.0   6.0   5.5   IR7   IR3

■   ■   ■   ■   ■

Menu: Layer→Merge Down

Mac: Cmd + E

Win: Ctrl + E

This command merges the target layer with the layer below it, as long as the layer below the target layer is visible and is a normal layer (not a type, adjustment, or fill layer). The name of the layer below the target layer is the name that is kept.

Merge All Visible Layers into the Target Layer

7.0   6.0   5.5   IR7   IR3

■   ■   ■   ■   ■

Menu: Layer→Merge Visible

Mac: Cmd + Shift + E

Win: Ctrl + Shift + E

This command merges all visible layers into the target layer. The name of the target layer is the name that is kept.

Merge a Copy of All Visible Layers into the Target Layer

7.0   6.0   5.5   IR7   IR3

■   ■   ■   ■   ■

Both: (Option) [Alt]+ Merge Visible

Mac: Cmd + Option + Shift + E

Win: Ctrl + Alt + Shift + E

This command merges a copy of all the visible layers into the target layer, leaving the original layers intact. However, this does change the target layer. What you might want to do instead is to create a composite copy of all visible layers into a new layer. To accomplish this, just do the obvious. Create a new layer before using this shortcut.

Layers

This is a great shortcut to use when making individual frames of an animation by hand. Each frame ends up being a composite of the individual layers. After you have the individual layers set up the way you want them for a particular animation frame, create a new empty layer, and use this shortcut. Modify the individual layers for the next frame, and repeat the process.

Merge All Linked Layers into the Target Layer   7.0   6.0   5.5   IR7   IR3
■ ■ ■ ■ ■

Menu: Layer→Merge Linked

Mac: Cmd + E

Win: Ctrl + E

This command merges all the linked layers into the target layer—as long as the linked layers are visible! If any of the linked layers are hidden, they are deleted. This is actually a great tip to effectively merge the layers you want to composite and delete the layers you don't want at the same time.

Merge a Copy of the Target Layer into the Layer Below
7.0   6.0   5.5   IR7   IR3
■ ■ ■ ■ ■

Mac: Cmd + Option + E or Option + Layer→Merge Down

Win: Ctrl + Alt + E or Alt + Layer→Merge Down

This command merges a copy of the target layer with the layer below it, as long as the layer below the target layer is visible.

Merge a Copy of All Linked Layers into the Target Layer
7.0   6.0   5.5   IR7   IR3
■ ■ ■ ■ ■

Mac: Cmd + Option + E or Option + Layers→Merge Linked

Win: Ctrl + Alt + E or Alt + Layers→Merge Linked

This command merges a copy of all the visible linked layers into the target layer.

Transparency Shortcuts

Toggle Preserve Transparency On and Off for Target Layer

7.0   6.0   5.5   IR7   IR3

Both: / (forward slash)

Load Layer Transparency as a Selection

7.0   6.0   5.5   IR7   IR3

Mac: Cmd + click layer in Layers Palette

Win: Ctrl + click layer in Layers Palette

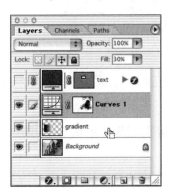

Add Layer Transparency to a Selection

7.0   6.0   5.5   IR7   IR3

Mac: Cmd + Shift + click layer in Layers Palette

Win: Ctrl + Shift + click layer in Layers Palette

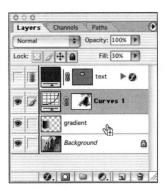

Layers

Subtract Layer Transparency from a Selection 7.0 6.0 5.5 IR7 IR3

■ ■ ■ ■ ■

Mac: Cmd + Option + click layer in Layers Palette

Win: Ctrl + Alt + click layer in Layers Palette

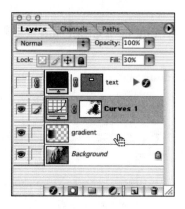

Intersect Layer Transparency with a Selection 7.0 6.0 5.5 IR7 IR3

■ ■ ■ ■ ■

Mac: Cmd + Option + Shift + click layer in Layers Palette

Win: Ctrl + Alt + Shift + click layer in Layers Palette

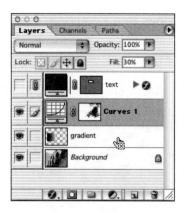

Layer Mask Commands

Create Layer Mask with Reveal All/Reveal Selection

7.0 6.0 5.5 IR7 IR3
■   ■   ■   ■   ■

Mouse: Click Layer Mask icon

Create Layer Mask with Hide All/Hide Selection

7.0 6.0 5.5 IR7 IR3
■   ■   ■   ■   ■

Mac: Option + click Layer Mask icon

Win: Alt + click Layer Mask icon

Create Layer Clipping Path with Reveal All/Reveal Current Path

7.0 6.0 5.5 IR7 IR3
■   ■   □   □   □

Mac: Cmd + click Layer Mask icon

Win: Ctrl + click Layer Mask icon

Create Layer Clipping Path with Hide All/Hide Current Path

7.0 6.0 5.5 IR7 IR3
■   ■   □   □   □

Mac: Cmd + Option + click Layer Mask icon

Win: Ctrl + Alt + click Layer Mask icon

Toggle Layer Mask or Layer Clipping Path On/Off

7.0 6.0 5.5 IR7 IR3

■   ■   ■   ■   ■

Mouse: Shift + click layer mask or layer clipping path thumbnail

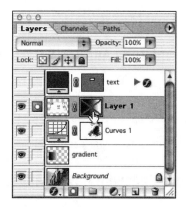

Toggle Between Layer Mask and Composite View

7.0 6.0 5.5 IR7 IR3

■   ■   ■   ■   ■

Mac: Option + click layer mask thumbnail

Win: Alt + click layer mask thumbnail

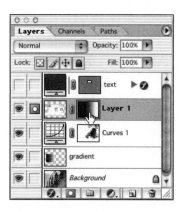

Make Layer Active When the Layer Mask Is Active

7.0 6.0 5.5 IR7 IR3

■ ■ ■ ■ ■

Mac: Cmd + ~ (tilde)

Win: Ctrl + ~ (tilde)

Make Layer Mask Active When the Layer Is Active

7.0 6.0 5.5 IR7 IR3

■ ■ ■ ■ ■

Mac: Cmd + \ (backslash key)

Win: Ctrl + \ (backslash key)

Load Layer Mask as a Selection

7.0 6.0 5.5 IR7 IR3

■ ■ ■ ■ □

Mac: Cmd + Option + \ (backslash key)

Win: Ctrl + Alt + \ (backslash key)

Toggle Rubylith (Mask Overlay) Mode for Layer Mask On/Off

7.0 6.0 5.5 IR7 IR3

■ ■ ■ ■ ■

Both: \ (backslash key)

Mac: Option + Shift + click layer mask thumbnail

Win: Alt + Shift + click layer mask thumbnail

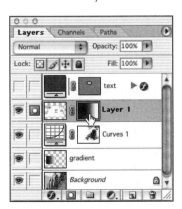

Layers

Link/Unlink a Layer Mask or Layer Clipping Path with Its Layer

7.0 6.0 5.5 IR7 IR3

■   ■   ■   ■   ■

Mouse: Click in the Link Layer Mask icon area (between the layer and the layer or layer clipping path)

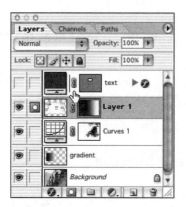

Open the Layer Mask Options Dialog Box

7.0 6.0 5.5 IR7 IR3

■   ■   ■   ■   ■

Mouse: Double-click the Layer Mask icon

Layer Effects Commands

Accessing Layer Effects Panels

7.0 6.0 5.5 IR7 IR3

□   □   ■   □   □

In Photoshop 5.5, after you have the Layer Effects Options dialog box open, you can quickly switch between the various panels using these shortcuts.

Panel	Mac	Win
Drop Shadow	Cmd + 1	Ctrl + 1
Inner Shadow	Cmd + 2	Ctrl + 2
Outer Glow	Cmd + 3	Ctrl + 3
Inner Glow	Cmd + 4	Ctrl + 4
Bevel and Emboss	Cmd + 5	Ctrl + 5

Panel	Mac	Win
Color Fill	Cmd + 6	Ctrl + 6
Next Effect	Cmd + N	Ctrl + N
Previous Effect	Cmd + P	Ctrl + P

Accessing Layer Styles Panels

7.0 6.0 5.5 IR7 IR3
■ □ □ □ □

In Photoshop 6 and 7, the Layer Effects dialog is now called the Layer Style dialog box, and there are a few new effects to choose from. After you have the Layer Style dialog box open, you can quickly switch between the various panels using these shortcuts.

Panel	Mac	Win
Drop Shadow	Cmd + 1	Ctrl + 1
Inner Shadow	Cmd + 2	Ctrl + 2
Outer Glow	Cmd + 3	Ctrl + 3
Inner Glow	Cmd + 4	Ctrl + 4
Bevel and Emboss	Cmd + 5	Ctrl + 5
Satin	Cmd + 6	Ctrl + 6
Color Overlay	Cmd + 7	Ctrl + 7
Gradient Overlay	Cmd + 8	Ctrl + 8
Pattern Overlay	Cmd + 9	Ctrl + 9
Stroke	Cmd + 0	Ctrl + 0

Clear Layer Effects

7.0 6.0 5.5 IR7 IR3
□ □ ■ □ □

Menu: Layer→Effects→Clear Effects

Mac: Option + double-click effect icon

Win: Alt + double-click effect icon

This shortcut removes one layer effect at a time, in the reverse order that you applied the effects to the layer.

Layers

In Photoshop 6 and 7, layer effects behave just like other layers—you can hide and show them, drag them to the trash, and so on.

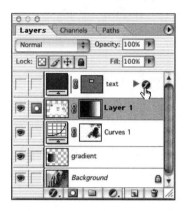

Edit Layer Effect (Style) Options

7.0 6.0 5.5 IR7 IR3

Menu: Layer→Effects→Choose the effect to edit

Mouse: Double-click effect icon

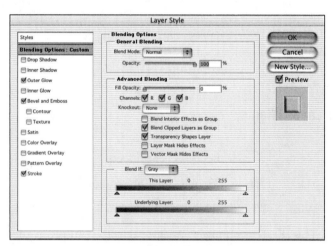

Toggle Effects (Styles) On/Off Without Dialog Box

7.0 6.0 5.5 IR7 IR3

■   ■   ■   □   □

Menu: Layer→Effects→desired effect

Mac: Option + menu item

Win: Alt + menu item

In Photoshop 6 and 7, you can just turn off the eyeball for the effect you want to hide.

Hide All Layer Effects (Styles) for a Layer but One

7.0 6.0 5.5 IR7 IR3

■   ■   ■   ■   ■

Mac: Option + click on style visibility icon

Win: Alt + click on style visibility icon

Use the modifier, and click on the layer visibility icon for the layer effect you want to keep visible. All the other layer styles for the layer will be turned off. The layer does not have to be active for this to work.

Reposition Effect (Style) While in Effect Dialog Box

7.0 6.0 5.5 IR7 IR3

■   ■   ■   □   □

Mouse: Drag in the image window (works for the Drop Shadow, Inner Shadow, Gradient Overlay, and Pattern Overlay effects).

Reposition Effect (Style) While in Effect Dialog Box Constrained to 45-Degree Axis

7.0 6.0 5.5 IR7 IR3

■   ■   ■   □   □

Mouse: Shift + drag in the image window

Type

Apply and Exit from the Type Dialog Box

7.0	6.0	5.5	IR7	IR3
☐	☐	■	☐	☐

Both: Enter, NOT Return

Edit Type Options

7.0	6.0	5.5	IR7	IR3
☐	☐	■	☐	☐

Both: Double-click Type icon or layer name

In Photoshop 6 and 7, you can just edit the text directly on the
canvas without the Type tool; however, double-clicking the type
icon is applicable to Photoshop 6 to start editing the type as well.
In Photoshop 7, you can double-click on the layer thumbnail of
the Type layer you want to edit. This will automatically switch you
to the Type tool and highlight all the type on that layer for you.

Reposition Type from Within the Type Dialog Box

7.0	6.0	5.5	IR7	IR3
☐	☐	■	☐	☐

Both: Press and drag in the image window

Photoshop 6 and ImageReady allow you to create and edit text
directly on the canvas. You can also reposition the type while
editing it in Photoshop 7 by moving the cursor outside the type
area and dragging.

Photoshop 5/5.5

Toggle to Eyedropper Tool

7.0 6.0 5.5 IR7 IR3
■ ■ ■ □ □

Mac: Option

Win: Alt

This shortcut allows you to choose a new foreground color from within the image (and the color for the text you are about to create) before entering the Type dialog box and without having to switch tools first. This shortcut works with the Vertical Type tool as well. In Photoshop 7, Option- or Alt-clicking with the Type tool allows you to numerically specify the dimensions of a paragraph text container.

Toggle the Text Mode Between Pixels and Mask

7.0 6.0 5.5 IR7 IR3
□ ■ □ □ □

Both: [or {

Photoshop 7 features dedicated tools for creating text and text masks.

Toggle the Text Orientation

7.0 6.0 5.5 IR7 IR3
□ ■ □ □ □

Photoshop 7 features dedicated tools for creating horizontal and vertical text.

Both:] or }

Character Selection Shortcuts

7.0 6.0 5.5 IR7 IR3
□ □ ■ □ □

	Mac	Win
One character to the right	Shift + Right Arrow	
One character to the left	Shift + Left Arrow	
One word to the right	Cmd + Shift + Right Arrow	Ctrl + Shift + Right Arrow
One word to the left	Cmd + Shift + Left Arrow	Ctrl + Shift + Left Arrow
One line up	Shift + Up Arrow	
One line down	Shift + Down Arrow	

Character Selection Shortcuts

6.0 5.5 5.0 IR3 IR2

These selection shortcuts were added in Photoshop 6.0:

	Mac	Win
To start of line	Shift + Home	
To end of line	Shift + End	
To start of current paragraph, and then to start of previous	Cmd + Shift + Up Arrow repeatedly	Ctrl + Shift + Up Arrow repeatedly
To end of current paragraph, and then to end of previous	Cmd + Shift + Down Arrow repeatedly	Ctrl + Shift + Down Arrow repeatedly
To start of story	Cmd + Shift + Home	Ctrl + Shift + Home
To end of story	Cmd + Shift + End	Ctrl + Shift + End

Select a Word

7.0 6.0 5.5 IR7 IR3

Mouse: Double-click word

Select a Line

7.0 6.0 5.5 IR7 IR3

Mouse: Triple-click word

Select a Paragraph

7.0 6.0 5.5 IR7 IR3

Mouse: Quadruple-click word

Select an Entire Story

7.0 6.0 5.5 IR7 IR3

Menu: Select→Select All

Mouse: Quadruple-click word

Type

Select Word and Then Select a Word at a Time

7.0	6.0	5.5	IR7	IR3
■	■	□	■	■

Mouse: Double-click and drag

Select Line and Then Select a Line at a Time

7.0	6.0	5.5	IR7	IR3
■	■	□	■	■

Mouse: Triple-click and drag

Select Paragraph and Then Select a Paragraph at a Time

7.0	6.0	5.5	IR7	IR3
■	■	□	■	■

Mouse: Quadruple-click and drag

Select All

7.0	6.0	5.5	IR7	IR3
■	■	■	■	■

Menu: Edit→Select All

Mac: Cmd + A

Win: Ctrl + A

In Photoshop 6 and 7 and ImageReady 3 and 7, you can also use the mouse to quintuple-click the text.

Select Characters from the Current Insertion Point

7.0	6.0	5.5	IR7	IR3
■	■	■	■	■

Both: Shift + click

Add to a Selection

7.0	6.0	5.5	IR7	IR3
■	■	■	□	□

Both: Shift + click then drag

This shortcut works with the Vertical Type Mask tool as well.

Subtract from a Selection

7.0 6.0 5.5 IR7 IR3

Mac: Option + click then drag

Win: Alt + click then drag

This shortcut works with the Vertical Type Mask tool as well.

Intersect with a Selection

7.0 6.0 5.5 IR7 IR3

Mac: Option + Shift + click then drag

Win: Alt + Shift + click then drag

This shortcut works with the Vertical Type Mask tool as well.

Show/Hide Type Selection

7.0 6.0 5.5 IR7 IR3

Mac: Cmd + H

Win: Ctrl + H

If you have type selected, the highlighting changes the color of the type. Use this shortcut to toggle the selection highlighting off and on so you can see the color applied to each character.

Cut, Copy, and Paste in the Type Dialog Box or a Selected Type Layer

7.0 6.0 5.5 IR7 IR3

Mac: Cmd + X, Cmd + C, Cmd + V

Win: Ctrl + X, Ctrl + C, Ctrl + V

Cursor Movement Shortcuts

7.0 6.0 5.5 IR7 IR3

	Mac	Win
One character right	Right Arrow	
One character left	Left Arrow	
One line up	Up Arrow	

...continues

	Mac	Win
One line down	Down Arrow	
One word right	Cmd + Right Arrow	Ctrl + Right Arrow
One word left	Cmd + Left Arrow	Ctrl + Left Arrow

Cursor Movement Shortcuts

7.0 6.0 5.5 IR7 IR3
■   ■   □   ■   ■

These cursor movement shortcuts have been added to 6.0:

	Mac	Win
To start of the line	Home	
To end of the line	End	
To the start of the next line	Cmd + Down Arrow	Ctrl + Down Arrow
To the start of story	Cmd + Home	Ctrl + Home
To the end of story	Cmd + End	Ctrl + End
To the start of the current paragraph, and then to the start of the previous paragraph	Cmd + Up Arrow repeatedly	Ctrl + Up Arrow repeatedly

Editing a Type Layer

7.0 6.0 5.5 IR7 IR3
□   □   ■   □   □

Mouse: Click the text with the Type tool

To edit a type layer, you usually double-click the name of the layer in the Layers palette. However, you can also open the Type dialog box for a given type layer by using the Type tool. If you click a transparent area with the Type tool, the Type dialog box opens, and whatever you type is placed on a new layer. If you click the actual type in the layer, the Type dialog box opens with that specific text in it so that you can edit the existing type layer.

Constrain as You Reposition Type from Within the Type Dialog Box

7.0 6.0 5.5 IR7 IR3
☐ ☐ ■ ☐ ☐

Mouse: Shift + click and drag in the image window

Paragraph Formatting Shortcuts

Text Alignment Shortcuts

7.0 6.0 5.5 IR7 IR3
■ ■ ■ ☐ ☐

With the text selected, use these easy shortcuts to make alignment changes. The ability to control the justification of the last line of a paragraph is new to Photoshop 6 and 7.

	Mac	Win
Left/Top	Cmd + Shift + L	Ctrl + Shift + L
Center	Cmd + Shift + C	Ctrl + Shift + C
Right/Bottom	Cmd + Shift + R	Ctrl + Shift + R
Justify with last line left	Cmd + Shift + J	Ctrl + Shift + J
Justify with last line force justified	Cmd + Shift + F	Ctrl + Shift + F

Toggle Hyphenation of Paragraph

7.0 6.0 5.5 IR7 IR3
■ ■ ☐ ☐ ☐

Mac: Cmd + Option + Shift + H

Win: Ctrl + Alt + Shift + H

Toggle Single- and Every-Line Composer

7.0 6.0 5.5 IR7 IR3
■ ■ ☐ ☐ ☐

Mac: Cmd + Option + Shift + T

Win: Ctrl + Alt + Shift + T

Type

Character Formatting Shortcuts

Text Point Size Adjustment Shortcuts

7.0 6.0 5.5 IR7 IR3

Your text must be selected to use these shortcuts:

	Mac	Win
Increase by 2 Points	Cmd + Shift + >	Ctrl + Shift + >
Decrease by 2 Points	Cmd + Shift + <	Ctrl + Shift + <
Increase by 10 Points	Cmd + Option + Shift + >	Ctrl + Alt + Shift + >
Decrease by 10 Points	Cmd + Option + Shift + <	Ctrl + Alt + Shift + <

Leading Adjustment Shortcuts

7.0 6.0 5.5 IR7 IR3

Your text must be selected for these shortcuts to work. Selecting Auto Leading using the keyboard was introduced in Photoshop 6 (but is not a feature of ImageReady).

	Mac	Win
Increase by 2 Points	Option + Down Arrow	Alt + Down Arrow
Decrease by 2 Points	Option + Up Arrow	Alt + Up Arrow
Increase by 10 Points	Cmd + Option + Down Arrow	Ctrl + Alt + Down Arrow
Decrease by 10 Points	Cmd + Option + Up Arrow	Ctrl + Alt + Up Arrow
Select Auto Leading	Cmd + Option + Shift + A	Ctrl + Alt + Shift+ A

Type

Character Formatting Shortcuts

Kerning/Tracking Adjustment Shortcuts

7.0 6.0 5.5 IR7 IR3
■   ■   ■   ■   ■

If your text is selected, then tracking will be applied to the entire selection. If the insertion point is between two characters, then that pair will be kerned. Selecting zero tracking using the keyboard is new to Photoshop 6 (but is not a feature of ImageReady 3).

	Mac	Win
Increase by 2/100 Em Space	Option + Right Arrow	Alt + Right Arrow
Decrease by 2/100 Em Space	Option + Left Arrow	Alt + Left Arrow
Increase by 10/100 Em Space	Cmd + Option + Right Arrow	Ctrl + Alt + Right Arrow
Decrease by 10/100 Em Space	Cmd + Option + Left Arrow	Ctrl + Alt + Left Arrow

Set Tracking to 0

7.0 6.0 5.5 IR7 IR3
■   ■   □   □   □

Mac: Cmd + Shift + Q

Win: Ctrl + Shift + Q

Note: Mac OS X reserves Cmd + Shift + Q for logging out the current user, so Photoshop 7 on OS X uses Cmd + Shift + 0 (zero) to set tracking to 0.

Toggle Underlining

7.0 6.0 5.5 IR7 IR3
■   ■   ■   □   □

Mac: Cmd + Shift + U

Win: Ctrl + Shift + U

Toggle All Uppercase

7.0 6.0 5.5 IR7 IR3
■   ■   ■   □   □

Mac: Cmd + Shift + K

Win: Ctrl + Shift + K

Type

Toggle Small Caps

7.0	6.0	5.5	IR7	IR3
■	■	■	☐	☐

Mac: Cmd + Shift + H

Win: Ctrl + Shift + H

Toggle Superscript

7.0	6.0	5.5	IR7	IR3
■	■	■	☐	☐

Mac: Cmd + Shift + + (plus sign)

Win: Ctrl + Shift + + (plus sign)

Toggle Subscript

7.0	6.0	5.5	IR7	IR3
■	■	■	☐	☐

Mac: Cmd + Option + Shift + + (plus sign)

Win: Ctrl + Alt + Shift + + (plus sign)

Set Horizontal Scale to 100%

7.0	6.0	5.5	IR7	IR3
■	■	☐	☐	☐

Mac: Cmd + Shift + X

Win: Ctrl + Shift + X

Set Vertical Scale to 100%

7.0	6.0	5.5	IR7	IR3
■	■	■	☐	☐

Mac: Cmd + Option + Shift + X

Win: Ctrl + Alt + Shift + X

The Select Menu

Selection Commands

Select All

	7.0	6.0	5.5	IR7	IR3
	■	■	■	■	■

Menu: Select→All

Mac: Cmd + A

Win: Ctrl + A

Deselect

	7.0	6.0	5.5	IR7	IR3
	■	■	■	■	■

Menu: Select→Deselect

Mac: Cmd + D

Win: Ctrl + D

Reselect

	7.0	6.0	5.5	IR7	IR3
	■	■	■	■	■

Menu: Select→Reselect

Mac: Cmd + Shift + D

Win: Ctrl + Shift + D

Inverse

7.0	6.0	5.5	IR7	IR3
■	■	■	■	■

Menu: Select→Inverse

Mac: Cmd + Shift + I

Win: Ctrl + Shift + I

Feather

7.0	6.0	5.5	IR7	IR3
■	■	■	■	■

Menu: Select→Feather

Mac: Cmd + Option + D

Win: Ctrl + Alt + D

Layer Transparencies and Selections

Load Layer Transparency as a Selection

7.0	6.0	5.5	IR7	IR3
■	■	■	■	■

Mac: Cmd + click layer

Win: Ctrl + click layer

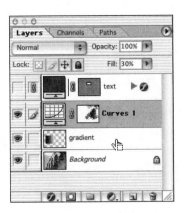

Add Layer Transparency to a Selection   7.0   6.0   5.5   IR7   IR3

Mac: Cmd + Shift + click layer

Win: Ctrl + Shift + click layer

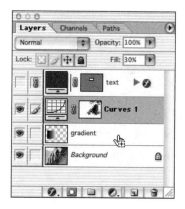

Subtract Layer Transparency from a Selection   7.0   6.0   5.5   IR7   IR3

Mac: Cmd + Option + click layer

Win: Ctrl + Alt + click layer

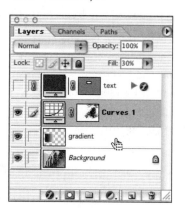

The Select Menu

Intersect Layer Transparency with a Selection 7.0 6.0 5.5 IR7 IR3

■ ■ ■ ■ ■

Mac: Cmd + Option + Shift + click layer

Win: Ctrl + Alt + Shift + click layer

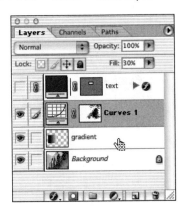

Creating Selections

Constrain to a Square Selection 7.0 6.0 5.5 IR7 IR3

■ ■ ■ ■ ■

Mouse: Shift + drag with the Rectangular Marquee tool

This shortcut works only if you are starting a new selection or adding Shift to a selection you are currently creating. If a selection already exists, you add to the selection instead. (See the shortcut to "Add a Square or Circle to Active Selection.")

Constrain to a Circle Selection 7.0 6.0 5.5 IR7 IR3

■ ■ ■ ■ ■

Mouse: Shift + drag with the elliptical marquee tool

This shortcut works only if you are starting a new selection or adding Shift to a selection you are currently creating. If a selection already exists, you add to the selection instead. (See the shortcut, "Add a Square or Circle to Active Selection.")

The Select Menu

Draw from the Center While Creating Selections

7.0   6.0   5.5   IR7   IR3

■   ■   ■   ■   ■

Mac: Option + drag

Win: Alt + drag

Normally, when creating a selection, the selection anchors itself
from wherever you click, creating the selection outward from that
position in a diagonal direction. With this shortcut, wherever you
click becomes the center of the selection as you create it. Also,
remember that this shortcut works only if you are starting a new
selection or when you add the modifier key after you have started
the selection. If a selection already exists, you subtract from the
selection instead.

Constrain and Draw from the Center While Creating Selections

7.0   6.0   5.5   IR7   IR3

■   ■   ■   ■   ■

Mac: Option + Shift + drag

Win: Alt + Shift + drag

Normally, when creating a selection, the selection anchors itself
from wherever you click, creating the selection outward from that
position in a diagonal direction. With this shortcut, wherever you
click becomes the center of the selection as you create it. Also,
remember that this shortcut works only if you are starting a new
selection or when you add the modifier keys to a selection you
have started. If a selection already exists, you are left with the
intersection of the selections instead.

Constrain a Selection as You Move It

7.0   6.0   5.5   IR7   IR3

■   ■   ■   ■   ■

Mouse: Shift + drag

Make sure the cursor is within the selection area and that you
press the mouse button down before you hold down the Shift key.
If you hold down the Shift key first, you will add to the selection
when you start dragging. If the cursor is outside the selected area,
you will start a new selection instead of moving the existing one.

The Select Menu

Reposition a Selection as You Create It

7.0 6.0 5.5 IR7 IR3
■ ■ ■ ■ ■

Both: Spacebar

This is one of my favorite shortcuts. Sometimes you are trying to select a specific shape in an image and halfway through dragging out the selection, you realize you didn't start in the right position. Rather than starting over, just hold down the Spacebar. This allows you to drag the marquee to a different position. When you are ready to continue with the selection, just let go of the Spacebar. Remember to keep the mouse button down until you are finished making the selection.

Modifying Selections

Add to a Selection

7.0 6.0 5.5 IR7 IR3
■ ■ ■ ■ ■

Mouse: Shift + drag

This shortcut is the same when using any of the selection tools: Rectangular Marquee, Elliptical Marquee, Magic Wand, or any of the Lasso tools.

Add a Square or Circle to Active Selection   7.0 6.0 5.5 IR7 IR3

Using the Rectangular or Elliptical Marquee tool, hold down Shift, click and start to drag, then release the Shift key, and press it down again. To add a square or circle to an active selection from the center of where you start clicking, start by holding down the Shift key, click and begin to drag, then release the Shift key, and press down the Shift and (Option) [Alt] keys.

Subtract from a Selection   7.0 6.0 5.5 IR7 IR3

Mac: Option + drag

Win: Alt + drag

This shortcut is the same when using any of the selection tools: Rectangular Marquee, Elliptical Marquee, Magic Wand, or any of the Lasso tools.

The Select Menu

Subtract a Square or Circle from Active Selection

7.0   6.0   5.5   IR7   IR3

■   ■   ■   ■   ■

Using the Rectangular or Elliptical Marquee tool, hold down
(Option) [Alt], click and start to drag, then press the Shift key.

Intersect with a Selection

7.0   6.0   5.5   IR7   IR3

■   ■   ■   ■   ■

Mac: Option + Shift + drag

Win: Alt + Shift + drag

This shortcut is the same when using any of the selection tools:
Rectangular Marquee, Elliptical Marquee, or any of the Lasso
tools. To use this shortcut with the Magic Wand tool, click
instead of drag.

The Select Menu

Duplicate a Selection

7.0   6.0   5.5   IR7   IR3
■ ■ ■ ■ ■

Mac: Option + drag with Move tool

Win: Alt + drag with Move tool

Moving Marquees and Selections

Move Selection Marquee 1 Pixel

7.0   6.0   5.5   IR7   IR3
■ ■ ■ ■ ■

Both: Arrow keys

Mouse: With a selection tool active, place cursor inside the selection, then press and drag

As long as a selection tool is active (Marquee, Lasso, Magic Wand), the arrow keys move just the selection marquee—not any pixels—one pixel in the direction of the arrow key you choose.

Move Selection Marquee 10 Pixels

7.0   6.0   5.5   IR7   IR3
■ ■ ■ ■ ■

Both: Shift + Arrow keys

Mouse: With a selection tool active, place cursor inside the selection, then press and drag

As long as a selection tool is active (Marquee, Lasso, Magic Wand), holding down the Shift key and then using the arrow keys moves a selection marquee 10 pixels in the direction of the arrow key you choose.

The Select Menu

Move Selected Pixels 1 Pixel

7.0 6.0 5.5 IR7 IR3
■   ■   ■   ■   ■

Menu: Edit→Transform→Numeric

Both: Arrow keys

Mouse: With the Move tool active, press and drag

As long as the Move tool is active, the arrow keys move selected pixels one pixel in the direction of the arrow key you choose. If any other tool is active, hold down the (Cmd) [Ctrl] key, and then use the arrow keys.

Move Selected Pixels 10 Pixels

7.0 6.0 5.5 IR7 IR3
■   ■   ■   ■   ■

Menu: Edit→Transform→Numeric

Both: Shift + Arrow keys

Mouse: With the Move tool active, press and drag

As long as the Move tool is active, holding down the Shift key and then pressing the arrow keys moves selected pixels 10 pixels in the direction of the arrow key you choose. If any other tool is active, hold down the (Cmd + Shift) [Ctrl + Shift] keys, and then use the arrow keys.

Center When Dragging from One File to Another

7.0 6.0 5.5 IR7 IR3
■   ■   ■   ■   ■

Mouse: Shift + drag from one document to the other

If you want the selection or layer from one document to end up in the middle of the document you are dragging it to, hold down the Shift key and drag the item to the target document. Let go of the mouse before letting go of the Shift key.

Note: If the canvas sizes of the two documents are the same, holding down the Shift key places the dragged item in the target document in the same position as the original document.

The Select Menu

Register Items When Dragging from One Document to Another

7.0   6.0   5.5   IR7   IR3
■   ■   ■   ■   ■

Mouse: Shift + drag from one document to the other

If you want the selection or layer from one document to end up in the same position in the target document you are dragging it to, make sure that they both have the same canvas size. Hold down the Shift key as you drag the item to the target document.

Selecting with the Lasso Tools

Toggle Between Polygonal Lasso and Lasso tool

7.0   6.0   5.5   IR7   IR3
■   ■   ■   ■   ■

Mac: Option + drag

Win: Alt + drag

Holding down the modifier while in one of these two tools will toggle you to the other. You must keep the modifier key held down while using the tool to keep the toggle active.

Add a Point

7.0   6.0   5.5   IR7   IR3
■   ■   ■   ■   ■

Mouse: Single-click

Delete the Last Point

7.0   6.0   5.5   IR7   IR3
■   ■   ■   ■   ■

Both: Delete

Close the Selection

7.0   6.0   5.5   IR7   IR3
■   ■   ■   ■   ■

Both: Double-click or Enter

The Select Menu

Close the Selection at the Starting Point

7.0 6.0 5.5 IR7 IR3
■   ■   ■   ■   ■

Mouse: Click on the starting point

Close the Selection Using a Straight-Line Segment

7.0 6.0 5.5 IR7 IR3
■   ■   ■   ■   ■

Mac: Option + double-click

Win: Alt + double-click

Cancel the Operation

7.0 6.0 5.5 IR7 IR3
■   ■   ■   ■   ■

Both: Escape

Mac: Cmd + . (period)

Win: Ctrl + . (period)

Adjust Magnetic Lasso Width

7.0 6.0 5.5 IR7 IR3
■   ■   ■   □   □

Increase	]
Decrease	[
Minimum Width	{
Maximum Width	}

Changes value in single pixel increments. Minimum value is
1 pixel; maximum value is 256 pixels.

Adjust Magnetic Lasso Edge Contrast

7.0 6.0 5.5 IR7 IR3
■   ■   ■   □   □

Increase	, (comma)
Decrease	. (period)
Minimum Edge Contrast	<
Maximum Edge Contrast	→

Changes value in 1% increments. Minimum value is 1%;
maximum value is 100%.

Adjust Magnetic Lasso Frequency

7.0	6.0	5.5	IR7	IR3
■	■	■	☐	☐

Increase	; (semi-colon)
Decrease	' (apostrophe)
Minimum Frequency	: (colon)
Maximum Frequency	" (quotation marks)

Changes value in single unit increments. Minimum value is 1; maximum value is 256.

Channel Commands

Show or Hide a Channel

7.0	6.0	5.5	IR7	IR3
■	■	■	☐	☐

Mouse: Click in Eye icon area

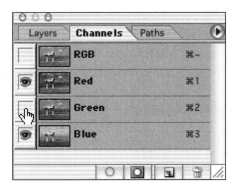

The Select Menu

The Select Menu

Target Individual Channels

7.0　6.0　5.5　IR7　IR3

■　■　■　□　□

Both:　Click desired channel thumbnail

Mac:　Cmd + [1–9]

Win:　Ctrl + [1–9]

With these shortcuts, you target an individual channel without having to use the Channels palette. Hold down the specified modifier key, and then press the number of the channel you want to target. For instance, in an RGB file, the first three channels in the file are the red, green, and blue channels, respectively. (Cmd + 1) [Ctrl + 1] targets the red channel, (Cmd + 2) [Ctrl + 2] targets the green channel, and so on. (Cmd + 4) [Ctrl + 4] targets the first of any alpha channels you have created in the file. You can target the first nine channels in the file using the 1–9 keys.

(Cmd + ~) [Ctrl + ~] targets the composite RGB channel. If a layer has a layer mask attached to it, (Cmd + \) [Ctrl + \] targets the layer mask of the active layer.

Note: If you click on the composite channel, this in effect turns on the individual channels that make up the composite channel.

Target the Composite Channel

7.0　6.0　5.5　IR7　IR3

■　■　■　□　□

Mac:　Cmd + ~ (tilde)

Win:　Ctrl + ~ (tilde)

To return to the composite channel, hold down the appropriate modifier key and press the tilde key—it's the key to the left of the number 1 key.

Create a New Channel

7.0　6.0　5.5　IR7　IR3

■　■　■　□　□

Mouse: Click the New Channel button

Clicking the New Channel button in the Channels palette skips the New Channel dialog box when creating a new channel. Channels are automatically named (Alpha 1, Alpha 2, and so on).

Create a New Channel with the New Channel Dialog Box

7.0 6.0 5.5 IR7 IR3

■ ■ ■ ☐ ☐

Mac: Option + click the New Channel button in the Channels palette

Win: Alt + click the New Channel button in the Channels palette

This shortcut opens the New Channel dialog box and gives you a chance to name the new channel and specify other options as well.

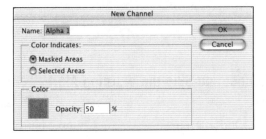

Duplicate a Channel

7.0 6.0 5.5 IR7 IR3

■ ■ ■ ☐ ☐

Mouse: Drag the channel to the New Channel button

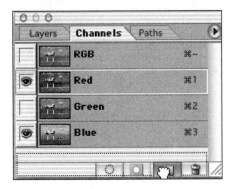

The Select Menu

Delete a Channel

7.0   6.0   5.5   IR7   IR3

Mouse: Click the Delete Channel button

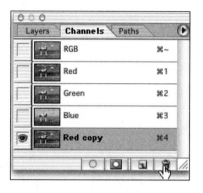

Delete a Channel and Skip the Warning Alert

7.0   6.0   5.5   IR7   IR3

Mac: Option + click the Delete Channel button

Win: Alt + click the Delete Channel button

Create a New Spot Color Channel

7.0   6.0   5.5   IR7   IR3

Mac: Cmd + click the New Channel button

Win: Ctrl + click the New Channel button

Save a Selection as a Channel

7.0 6.0 5.5 IR7 IR3

■ ■ ■ ■ ■

Menu: Select→Save Selection

Mouse: Click the Save Selection button

Clicking the Save Selection button in the Channels palette skips the New Channel dialog box when creating a new channel. Channels are automatically named (Alpha 1, Alpha 2, and so on).

Load a Channel as a Selection

7.0 6.0 5.5 IR7 IR3

■ ■ ■ ■ ■

Menu: Select→Load Selection

Mac: Cmd + Option + [1–9] or Cmd + click on the desired channel

Win: Ctrl + Alt + [1–9] or Ctrl + click on the desired channel

Mouse: Target desired channel and then click Load Channel as Selection button

With these shortcuts, you can load an individual channel as a selection without having to use the Channels palette. Hold down the specified modifier keys, and then press the number of the channel you want to load. For instance, in an RGB file, the first three channels in the file are the red, green, and blue channels, respectively. (Cmd + Option + 1) [Ctrl + Alt + 1] loads the red channel, (Cmd + Option + 2) [Ctrl + Alt + 2] loads the green channel, and so on. (Cmd + Option + 4) [Ctrl +Alt + 4] loads the first of any alpha channels you have created in the file. You can load the first nine channels in the file using the 1–9 keys. ImageReady provides only the menu method to load a channel as a selection.

(Cmd + Option + \) [Ctrl + Alt + \] will load the active layer's layer mask as a selection.

The Select Menu

The Select Menu

Save a Selection as a Channel with the New Channel Dialog Box

7.0 6.0 5.5 IR7 IR3

Menu: Select→Save Selection

Mac: Option + click the Save Selection button

Win: Alt + click the Save Selection button

This shortcut opens the New Channel dialog box and gives you a chance to name the new channel and specify other options as well.

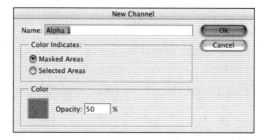

Add a Channel to a Selection

7.0 6.0 5.5 IR7 IR3

Menu: Select→Load Selection

Both: Shift + click the Load Selection button

Mac: Cmd + Shift + click the channel thumbnail

Win: Ctrl + Shift + click the channel thumbnail

Subtract a Channel from a Selection

7.0   6.0   5.5   IR7   IR3

■   ■   ■   □   □

Menu: Select→Load Selection

Mac: Cmd + Option + click the channel thumbnail or Option + click the Load Selection button

Win: Ctrl + Alt + click the channel thumbnail or Alt + click the Load Selection button

Intersect a Channel with a Selection

7.0   6.0   5.5   IR7   IR3

■   ■   ■   □   □

Menu: Select→Load Selection

Mac: Cmd + Option + Shift + click the channel thumbnail or Option + Shift + click the Load Selection button

Win: Ctrl + Alt + Shift + click the channel thumbnail or Alt + Shift + click the Load Selection button

The Select Menu

View a Color Channel Without Hiding Other Color Channels

7.0 6.0 5.5 IR7 IR3

■ ■ ■ ☐ ☐

Mouse: Shift + click the channel name

Edit Channel Options

7.0 6.0 5.5 IR7 IR3

■ ■ ■ ☐ ☐

Mouse: Double-click on the desired channel

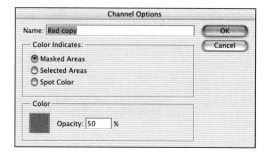

Path Commands

Create a New Path

7.0 6.0 5.5 IR7 IR3

■ ■ ■ ☐ ☐

Mouse: Click the New Path button

Clicking the New Path button in the Paths palette skips the New Path dialog box when creating a new path. Paths are automatically named (Path 1, Path 2, and so on).

Create a New Path with the New Path Dialog Box

7.0　6.0　5.5　IR7　IR3

■　■　■　☐　☐

Mac:　Option + click the New Path button in the Paths palette

Win:　Alt + click the New Path button in the Paths palette

This shortcut opens the New Path dialog box and gives you a chance to name the new path as you create it.

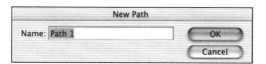

Duplicate a Path

7.0　6.0　5.5　IR7　IR3

■　■　■　☐　☐

Mouse: Drag path to the New Path button

Rename a Path While Duplicating It

7.0　6.0　5.5　IR7　IR3

■　■　■　☐　☐

Mac:　Option + drag path to the New Path button

Win:　Alt + drag path to the New Path button

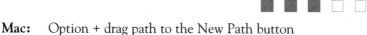

Delete a Path

7.0 6.0 5.5 IR7 IR3

Mouse: Click the Delete Path button

Delete a Path and Skip the Warning Alert

7.0 6.0 5.5 IR7 IR3

Mac: Option + click the Delete Path button

Win: Alt + click the Delete Path button

Draw Path Constrained to 45-Degree Axis

7.0 6.0 5.5 IR7 IR3

Mouse: Shift + click/drag

Add or Delete Anchor Points

7.0 6.0 5.5 IR7 IR3

Mouse: Click on path or anchor points

Photoshop 6.0 also has the Auto Add/Delete option for path tools to turn this on or off.

Select Multiple Anchor Points with Direct Select Tool

7.0 6.0 5.5 IR7 IR3

Mouse: Shift + click

Alternatively, if you are using the Pen tool, you can hold down the (Command) [Control] key to temporarily switch to the Direct Select tool.

The Select Menu

Edit a Pathname   7.0 6.0 5.5 IR7 IR3
                                       ■   ■   ■   □   □

> **Mouse:** Double-click pathname

Add a Path to a Selection   7.0 6.0 5.5 IR7 IR3
                                       ■   ■   ■   □   □

Mac: Cmd + Shift + click the path thumbnail

Win: Ctrl + Shift + click the path thumbnail

Subtract a Path from a Selection   7.0 6.0 5.5 IR7 IR3
                                       ■   ■   ■   □   □

Mac: Cmd + Option + click the path thumbnail

Win: Ctrl + Alt + click the path thumbnail

The Select Menu

Path Commands

Intersect a Path with a Selection

7.0   6.0   5.5   IR7   IR3

Mac: Cmd + Option + Shift + click the path thumbnail

Win: Ctrl + Alt + Shift + click the path thumbnail

Stroke a Path with the Foreground Color

7.0   6.0   5.5   IR7   IR3

Mouse: Click the Stroke Path button

Stroke a Path with the Foreground Color with the Stroke Path
Dialog Box   7.0 6.0 5.5 IR7 IR3

■ ■ ■ ☐ ☐

Mac: Option + click the Stroke Path button

Win: Alt + click the Stroke Path button

This shortcut opens the Stroke Path dialog box and allows you to specify which tool setting you want used to apply the stroke to the path.

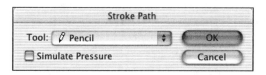

Fill a Path with the Foreground Color   7.0 6.0 5.5 IR7 IR3

■ ■ ■ ☐ ☐

Mouse: Click the Fill Path button

Fill a Path with the Foreground Color with the Fill Path
Dialog Box   7.0 6.0 5.5 IR7 IR3

■ ■ ■ ☐ ☐

Mac: Option + click the Fill Path button

Win: Alt + click the Fill Path button

This shortcut opens the Fill Path dialog box and allows you to specify fill options such as opacity, blend mode, feathering, and so on.

Convert Work Path into a Saved Path   7.0 6.0 5.5 IR7 IR3

■ ■ ■ ☐ ☐

Mouse: Double-click on the pathname or drag Work Path to the New Path button

The Select Menu

The Select Menu

Load Path as a Selection

7.0 6.0 5.5 IR7 IR3
■   ■   ■   □   □

Both: Enter or click the Load Selection button

Mac: Cmd + click the path thumbnail

Win: Ctrl + click the path thumbnail

Convert Path into a Selection with the Make Selection Dialog Box

7.0 6.0 5.5 IR7 IR3
■   ■   ■   □   □

Mac: Option + click the Load Selection button

Win: Alt + click the Load Selection button

This shortcut opens the Make Selection dialog box and allows you to specify options for the selection, such as a feathering radius.

Convert Selection into a Path

7.0 6.0 5.5 IR7 IR3
■   ■   ■   □   □

Mouse: Click the Make Work Path button

Convert Selection into a Path with the Work Path Dialog Box

	7.0	6.0	5.5	IR7	IR3
	■	■	■	□	□

Mac: Option + click the Make Work Path button

Win: Alt + click the Make Work Path button

This shortcut opens the Make Work Path dialog box and allows you to specify options for the path.

Add a Point

	7.0	6.0	5.5	IR7	IR3
	■	■	■	□	□

Mouse: Single-click

Delete the Last Point

	7.0	6.0	5.5	IR7	IR3
	■	■	■	□	□

Both: Delete

Close the Path

	7.0	6.0	5.5	IR7	IR3
	■	■	■	□	□

Both: Double-click or Enter

Close the Path at the Starting Point

	7.0	6.0	5.5	IR7	IR3
	■	■	■	□	□

Mouse: Click on the starting point

Close the Path Using a Straight-Line Segment

	7.0	6.0	5.5	IR7	IR3
	■	■	■	□	□

Mac: Option + double-click

Win: Alt + double-click

The Select Menu

Cancel the Operation

7.0	6.0	5.5	IR7	IR3
■	■	■	□	□

Both:	Escape
Mac:	Cmd + . (period)
Win:	Ctrl + . (period)

Switch to the Convert Point Tool

7.0	6.0	5.5	IR7	IR3
■	■	■	□	□

Mac:	Option + drag
Win:	Alt + drag

Adjust Magnetic Pen Width

7.0	6.0	5.5	IR7	IR3
■	■	■	□	□

Increase	]
Decrease	[
Minimum Width	{
Maximum Width	}

In Photoshop 7, the Magnetic Pen functionality is now an option of the Freeform Pen tool. You access it by selecting the Freeform Pen tool and turning on the Magnetic check box in the Options bar.

Adjust Magnetic Pen Edge Contrast

7.0	6.0	5.5	IR7	IR3
■	■	■	□	□

Increase	, (comma)
Decrease	. (period)
Minimum Edge Contrast	<
Maximum Edge Contrast	→

Adjust Magnetic Pen Frequency

7.0	6.0	5.5	IR7	IR3
■	■	■	□	□

Increase	; (semi-colon)
Decrease	' (apostrophe)
Minimum Frequency	: (colon)
Maximum Frequency	" (quotation marks)

The Filter Menu

Repeat the Last Filter Used

7.0 6.0 5.5 IR7 IR3
■   ■   ■   ■   ■

Menu: Filter→Name of the filter

Mac: Cmd + F

Win: Ctrl + F

This shortcut applies the last filter you used again; it does not reopen the dialog box of the filter you used last so that you can change the settings before applying again. As you might guess, a separate shortcut is available for that as well. Also note that this shortcut works only during the current Photoshop session—once you quit the application, Photoshop won't recall the last filter you used when you relaunch.

Reopen the Last Filter Used with Same Settings

7.0 6.0 5.5 IR7 IR3
■   ■   ■   ■   ■

Mac: Cmd + Option + F

Win: Ctrl + Alt + F

Fade the Last Filter Used

7.0 6.0 5.5 IR7 IR3
□   □   ■   □   □

Menu: Filter→Fade name of the filter

Mac: Cmd + Shift + F

Win: Ctrl + Shift + F

This is a great shortcut to knock back the intensity of a particular effect by playing with the opacity or the blend mode of the applied filter effect. In Photoshop 6 and 7, the Fade command can also apply to brush strokes and other edits. (In these versions, you'll find the menu item under the Edit menu.)

Extract, Liquify, and Pattern Maker Commands

Extract   7.0 6.0 5.5 IR7 IR3
                                                          ■   ■   ■   □   □

Menu: Filter→Extract

Mac: Cmd + Option + X

Win: Ctrl + Alt + X

(In Photoshop 5.5 and 6.0, the Extract command is located under the Image menu.)

Tool	Icon	Shortcut
Edge Highlighter		B
Fill		K (5.5)
		G (6)
Eraser		E
Eyedropper		I
Cleanup		C
Edge Touchup		T
Zoom		Z
Hand		H

Note: All other standard brush shortcuts work here as well, such as using the bracket keys to increase or decrease brush size, and so on.

Reverse Extract Tool Behavior   7.0 6.0 5.5 IR7 IR3
                                                          ■   ■   ■   □   □

Mac: Option

Win: Alt

For example, if you are using the Edge Highlighter tool, this shortcut switches you to the Eraser tool.

Liquify

7.0	6.0	5.5	IR7	IR3
■	■	□	□	□

Menu: Filter→Liquify

Mac: Cmd + Shift + X

Win: Ctrl + Shift + X

Note: In Photoshop 6, the Liquify command is located under the Image menu.

Tool	Icon	Shortcut
Warp		W
Turbulence		A
Twirl Clockwise		R
Twirl Counterclockwise		L
Pucker		P
Bloat		B
Shift Pixels		S
Reflection		M
Reconstruction		E
Freeze		F
Thaw Tool		T
Zoom Tool		Z
Hand Tool		H

...continues

Commands	Mac	Windows
Temporarily activate Hand tool	Spacebar	Spacebar
Zoom Out with Zoom tool selected	Option	Alt
Zoom In with any tool selected	Cmd + Spacebar	Ctrl + Spacebar
Zoom Out with any tool selected	Option + Spacebar	Option + Spacebar
Zoom In one level	Cmd + + (Plus)	Ctrl + + (Plus)
Zoom Out one level	Cmd + - (minus)	Ctrl + - (minus)
Zoom tool	Z	Z
Hand tool	H	H

Pattern Maker

7.0   6.0   5.5   IR7   IR3

Menu: Image→Pattern Maker

Mac: Cmd + Opt + Shift + X

Win: Ctrl + Alt + Shift + X

Tool	Mac	Windows
Marquee tool	M	M
Zoom tool	Z	Z
Hand tool	H	H
Change Cancel to Reset	Option	Alt
Generate or Generate Again	Cmd + G	Ctrl + G
Temporarily activate Hand tool	Spacebar	Spacebar
Zoom Out with Zoom tool selected	Option	Alt
Zoom In with any tool selected	Cmd + Spacebar	Ctrl + Spacebar
Zoom Out with any tool selected	Option + Spacebar	Option + Spacebar
Toggle Show Original and Show Generated	X	X

The following commands apply only when viewing the original image:

Command	Mac	Win
Select All	Cmd + A	Ctrl + A
Deselect All	Cmd + D	Ctrl + D
Undo/Redo	Cmd + Z	Ctrl + Z
Nudge selection left	Left Arrow	Left Arrow
Nudge selection right	Right Arrow	Right Arrow
Nudge selection down	Down Arrow	Down Arrow
Nudge selection up	Up Arrow	Up Arrow
Nudge selection by 10 pixels	Shift + direction arrow	Shift + direction arrow

The following commands apply only when viewing generated patterns:

Command	Mac	Win
Tile History: Go to first	Home	Home
Tile History: Go to previous	Left Arrow, Page Up	Left Arrow, Page Up
Tile History: Go to next	Right Arrow, Page Down	Right Arrow, Page Down
Tile History: Delete	Delete key	Backspace key

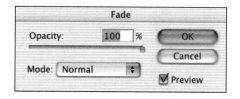

3D Transform Filter

3D Transform Filter

	7.0	6.0	5.5	IR7	IR3
	■	■	■	□	□

Menu: Render→3D Transform

Tool	Icon	Shortcut
Selection		V
Direct Selection		A
Cube		M
Sphere		N
Cylinder		C
Convert Anchor Point		
Add Anchor Point		+
Delete Anchor Point		-
Pan Camera		E
Trackball		R
Hand		H
Zoom		Z

Pan Image

	7.0	6.0	5.5	IR7	IR3
	■	■	■	■	■

Mouse: Spacebar + drag

Zoom In

	7.0	6.0	5.5	IR7	IR3
	■	■	■	■	■

Mac: Cmd + Spacebar + click/drag

Win: Ctrl + Spacebar + click/drag

Zoom Out

7.0 6.0 5.5 IR7 IR3

■   ■   ■   ■   ■

Mac: Option + Spacebar + click/drag

Win: Alt + Spacebar + click/drag

Lighting Effects Filter

Duplicate Light in Lighting Effects Preview

7.0 6.0 5.5 IR7 IR3

■   ■   ■   ■   ■

Mac: Option + drag light

Win: Alt + drag light

Delete Light in Lighting Effects Preview

7.0 6.0 5.5 IR7 IR3

■   ■   ■   ■   ■

Both: Delete

Adjust Light Footprint Without Changing the Angle

7.0 6.0 5.5 IR7 IR3

■   ■   ■   ■   ■

Mouse: Shift + drag handle

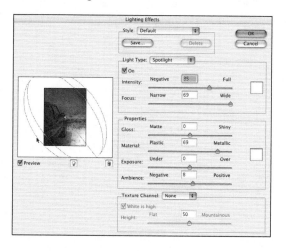

Adjust Light Angle Without Changing the Footprint

Mac: Cmd + drag handle

Win: Ctrl + drag handle

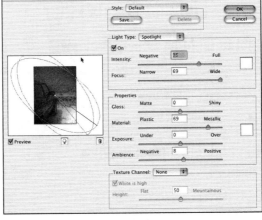

Preview Gamut Warning

7.0	6.0	5.5	IR7	IR3
■	■	■	☐	☐

Menu: View→Gamut Warning

Mac: Cmd + Shift + Y

Win: Ctrl + Shift + Y

Preview Browser Dither

7.0	6.0	5.5	IR7	IR3
☐	☐	☐	■	■

Menu: View→Preview→Browser Dither

Mac: Cmd + Shift + Y

Win: Ctrl + Shift + Y

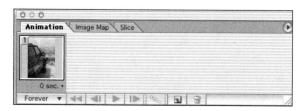

Preview CMYK

7.0	6.0	5.5	IR7	IR3
☐	☐	■	☐	☐

Menu: View→Preview→CMYK

Mac: Cmd + Y

Win: Ctrl + Y

Proof Colors

7.0	6.0	5.5	IR7	IR3
■	■	☐	☐	☐

Menu: View→Proof Colors

Mac: Cmd + Y

Win: Ctrl + Y

Toggle Between Document Preview Tabs

7.0	6.0	5.5	IR7	IR3
☐	☐	☐	■	■

Menu: View→Show Original/Optimized/2-Up/4-Up

Mac: Cmd + Y

Win: Ctrl + Y

This shortcut toggles you among the Original, Optimized, 2-Up, and 4-Up tabs in the ImageReady document window.

Toggle Through Gamma Previews in the Selected Image Pane 6.0

7.0	6.0	5.5	IR7	IR3
☐	☐	☐	■	■

Menu: View→Preview→Preview choice

Mac: Cmd + Option + Y

Win: Ctrl + Alt + Y

Hide Edges

7.0	6.0	5.5	IR7	IR3
☐	☐	■	☐	☐

Menu: View→Hide Edges

Mac: Cmd + H

Win: Ctrl + H

Hide Extras

7.0 6.0 5.5 IR7 IR3
■   ■   □   □   □

Menu: View→Show Extras

Mac: Cmd + H

Win: Ctrl + H

In Photoshop 6 and 7, this shortcut hides all the items in the
View→Show menu: Selection, Target Path, Grid, Guides,
Annotations, and Slices. In Photoshop 6, this command is also
listed as View→Hide Extras, and in Photoshop 7, it has been
renamed simply Extras with a checkbox to indicate visibility. By
default, they are all checked, and only checked items are toggled
by this command. Unchecked items are manually toggled as they
have been in previous versions. (The extras that need to be manually toggled have angle brackets in the menu to indicate this, such
as <Guides>.)

Hide Path

7.0 6.0 5.5 IR7 IR3
■   ■   ■   □   □

Menu: View→Hide Path

Mac: Cmd + Shift + H

Win: Ctrl + Shift + H

Show or Hide Slices

7.0 6.0 5.5 IR7 IR3
□   □   □   ■   ■

Both: Q

In Photoshop 6 and 7, the Hide Extras command (Cmd + H) [Ctrl
+ H] also hides/shows slice guides.

Show or Hide Rulers

7.0 6.0 5.5 IR7 IR3
■   ■   ■   ■   ■

Menu: View→Show/Hide Rulers

Mac: Cmd + R

Win: Ctrl + R

The View Menu

Show or Hide Guides

7.0	6.0	5.5	IR7	IR3
■	□	■	□	□

Menu: View→Show/Hide Guides

Mac: Cmd + ; (semicolon)

Win: Ctrl + ; (semicolon)

Show or Hide Guides

7.0	6.0	5.5	IR7	IR3
□	■	□	□	□

Menu: View→Show/Hide Guides

Mac: Cmd + ' (apostrophe)

Win: Ctrl + ' (apostrophe)

Toggle Snap

7.0	6.0	5.5	IR7	IR3
■	□	■	□	□

Menu: View→Snap to Guides

Mac: Cmd + Shift + ; (semicolon)

Win: Ctrl + Shift + ; (semicolon)

Toggle Snap

7.0	6.0	5.5	IR7	IR3
□	■	□	□	■

Menu: View→Snap to Guides

Mac: Cmd + ; (semicolon)

Win: Ctrl + ; (semicolon)

In Photoshop 6, (Cmd + ;) [Ctrl + ;] toggles the Snap command or whatever is checked in the View→Snap To menu.

Lock or Unlock Guides

7.0	6.0	5.5	IR7	IR3
■	■	■	■	■

Menu: View→Lock Guides

Mac: Cmd + Option + ; (semicolon)

Win: Ctrl + Alt + ; (semicolon)

Toggle Show/Hide Grid

7.0	6.0	5.5	IR7	IR3
☐	☐	■	☐	☐

Menu: View→Show Grid

Mac: Cmd + ' (apostrophe)

Win: Ctrl + ' (apostrophe)

Toggle Show/Hide Grid

7.0	6.0	5.5	IR7	IR3
☐	■	☐	☐	☐

Menu: View→Show→Show Grid

Mac: Cmd + Option + ' (apostrophe)

Win: Ctrl + Alt + ' (apostrophe)

Toggle Show/Hide Grid

7.0	6.0	5.5	IR7	IR3
■	☐	☐	☐	☐

Menu: View→Show→Show Grid

Mac: Cmd + "

Win: Ctrl + "

Toggle Snap to Grid

7.0	6.0	5.5	IR7	IR3
☐	☐	■	☐	☐

Menu: View→Snap to Grid

Mac: Cmd + Shift + ' (apostrophe)

Win: Ctrl + Shift + ' (apostrophe)

Toggle Snap to Grid

7.0	6.0	5.5	IR7	IR3
■	■	☐	☐	☐

Menu: View→Snap to Grid

Mac: (Cmd + ;)

Win: [Ctrl + ;]

Toggles the Snap command for guides, grid, slices, and document bounds.

Snap Guide to Ruler

7.0 6.0 5.5 IR7 IR3
■   ■   ■   ■   ■

Mouse: Shift + drag guide

Toggle Guide Orientation

7.0 6.0 5.5 IR7 IR3
■   ■   ■   ■   ■

Mac: Option + drag guide

Win: Alt + drag guide

The Window Menu

Close All Documents

Menu: Window→Close All

Mac: Cmd + Shift + W

Win: Ctrl + Shift + W

Note: Many of the following shortcuts list an F key. Some OS configurations may have reserved functionality for the F keys that supersede Photoshop's claim to the keys. For example, on a typical Macintosh laptop, you have to hold down the Fn (Function) key along with the desired Photoshop F key by default to get it to work. You may want to change the keyboard settings for your OS if that is the case for you.

Show or Hide the Optimize Palette

7.0 6.0 5.5 IR7 IR3

Menu: Window→Show/Hide Optimize

Both: F10

Show or Hide the Info Palette

7.0 6.0 5.5 IR7 IR3

Menu: Window→Show/Hide Info

Both: F8

Show or Hide the Options Palette

7.0 6.0 5.5 IR7 IR3

Menu: Window→Show/Hide Options

Both: Enter or Return

Mouse: Double-click on a tool

Show or Hide the Color Palette

7.0	6.0	5.5	IR7	IR3
■	■	■	■	■

Menu: Window→Show/Hide Color

Both: F6

Show or Hide the Swatches Palette

7.0	6.0	5.5	IR7	IR3
■	■	■	■	■

Menu: Window→Show/Hide Swatches

Both: F6

F6 shows or hides the Color palette. Also use it to show or hide the Swatches palette if you haven't changed the default grouping of the Color and Swatches palettes. To show Swatches if the Color palette is not open, press F6, and then click on the Swatches tab. To hide both the Swatches and the Color palettes, press the F6 key until they both disappear.

Show or Hide the Brushes Palette

7.0	6.0	5.5	IR7	IR3
■	□	■	□	□

Menu: Window→Show/Hide Brushes

Both: F5

Show or Hide the Layers Palette

7.0	6.0	5.5	IR7	IR3
■	■	■	■	■

Menu: Window→Show/Hide Layers

Both: F7

Show or Hide the Channels Palette

7.0 6.0 5.5 IR7 IR3

Menu: Window→Show/Hide Channels

Both: F7

F7 shows or hides the Layers palette. Also use it to show or hide the Channels palette if you haven't changed the default grouping of the Layers and Channels palettes. To show Channels if the Layers palette is not open, press F7, and then click on the Channels tab. To hide both the Channels and the Layers palettes, press the F7 key until they both disappear.

Show or Hide the Animation Palette

7.0 6.0 5.5 IR7 IR3

Menu: Window→Show/Hide Animation

Both: F11

Show or Hide the Slice Palette

7.0 6.0 5.5 IR7 IR3

Menu: Window→Show/Hide Slice

Both: F11

F11 shows or hides the Animation palette. Also use it to show or hide the Slice palette if you haven't changed the default grouping of the Animation and Slice palettes. To show Slice if the Animation palette is not open, press F11, and then click on the Slice tab. To hide both the Slice and the Animation palettes, press the F11 key until they both disappear.

The Window Menu

The Window Menu

Show or Hide the Rollover Palette

7.0 6.0 5.5 IR7 IR3

☐ ☐ ☐ ■ ■

Menu: Window→Show/Hide Rollover

Both: F11

F11 shows or hides the Animation palette. Also use it to show or hide the Rollover palette if you haven't changed the default grouping of the Animation and Rollover palettes. To show Rollover if the Animation palette is not open, press F11, and then click on the Rollover tab. To hide both the Rollover and the Animation palettes, press the F11 key until they both disappear.

Cycle Through Open Documents

7.0 6.0 5.5 IR7 IR3

■ ■ ■ ■ ■

Menu: Window→Choose open document

Both: Ctrl + Tab

In Photoshop 7, documents are listed under the Window→Documents submenu.

Steal the Attributes of an Open Document

7.0 6.0 5.5 IR7 IR3

■ ■ ■ ☐ ☐

Menu: Window→Choose the document from the list

Here is another one of those deeply buried, not obvious, and undocumented shortcuts that makes you say, "Doh! I wish I'd known that years ago!" When you are compositing images, it is often useful to make the canvas sizes of all the documents you are using the same. Three different places you can take advantage of this trick are the New dialog box, the Image Size dialog box, and the Canvas Size dialog box. When in any of these three places, you might have never noticed that most of the menus are grayed out and unavailable. However, the Window menu is available. If you choose any open document listed in the Window menu, Photoshop automatically changes the attributes of the New, Image Size, and Canvas Size dialog boxes to match the open document.

Actions

Photoshop 7 Power Shortcuts would be incomplete if I didn't mention the capability to create your own custom shortcuts using Actions. Actions first arrived in Photoshop 4. Photoshop 5 vastly improved what Actions could do by increasing the number of things that can be recorded. Just about everything can be recorded, with a few notable exceptions. My favorite improvement—changing a layer's blend mode and opacity—can now be recorded. You can use Actions to assign an F key (Function key) to any menu command that doesn't already have one, and you can use Actions to record many steps and then play back those steps on a batch of files.

In addition to the actual keyboard shortcuts for the Actions palette, here are 10 general tips to help you when you're working with Actions.

Top Ten Action Tips

1. When you record an Action, Photoshop records what hap-pened—not what you did. For instance, when you record the Select All command, you see "Set Selection" listed in the Action commands list. In other words, you need to learn to speak "Actionese." It is often helpful to click the triangle next to each command in the Action list to see the contents of an Action for it to make sense. In the previous Set Selection example, if you turn down the arrow, you see that it says, "To: All."

2. Actions are literal! That means if you select a layer by click-ing its layer name in the Layers palette, the name of the layer is recorded as well. This can cause problems on playback. For instance, if you record clicking a layer named bob and the file you play the Action back in does not have a layer in it named bob, your Action will not work like you wanted it to. Most of the time, it is better to record layers by their relative, or ordinal, position and not their name, so use the keyboard shortcuts to select and move layers. (See the "Layers" chapter if you need a reminder.)

3. To save your Actions so that they can be shared across platforms, make sure they are named with the .atn file extension.

4. If your Actions require a specific start state to work correctly, such as the image must be in the RGB mode, be sure to make a note of this some way. The easiest way to do this is to include a comment in the Action's name. For more complex situations, insert a Stop command, and enter a comment. When the Action is played, a dialog box appears with the text you entered.

5. You can record image adjustments (from the Image > Adjust menu) that rely on saved settings, such as Curves or Levels saved settings. In those instances, the Action records the pathname to the file you saved or loaded while you were recording. However, if you want to distribute the Action without those accompanying saved files, you have to trick Photoshop into embedding the saved settings.

    To do this—say, for the example of a Curves setting loaded from disk—double-click the Curves command in the Action. Add a point to the curve, and then click OK. Repeat this process, except delete the curve point you added previously; the Action now contains a complete description of the loaded curve. Similar workarounds work for other adjustments.

6. To re-record an Action step, just double-click it.

7. If you just want to have a particular dialog box appear (such as Gaussian Blur) so that you can enter your own values, don't record opening the dialog box from its menu. Instead, use Insert Menu Command. This opens a dialog box for you to type the menu command you want. You can also just choose the menu command you want from the actual menu, and it inserts the command for you.

8. To play a single step of an Action, hold down the (Cmd) [Ctrl] key, and double-click it.

9. To make the Batch command work faster, change the Cache Levels setting to 1 in the Image Cache Preferences, and turn off the History palette's automatic snapshot feature. (Note: Special thanks to Deke McClelland for that tip.) In 6.0, you can even record the setting of preferences, including this one.

10. The Move tool looks like it doesn't get recorded because you don't see any Action listed in the command list after you've moved something. To make the Move command appear in the command list, you have to do something else first. This is because Photoshop is waiting to see if you are going to move the layer or selection somewhere else before moving on to your next step, so it will only record a single move command and not all the smaller moves you made.

Action Commands

Select Multiple Commands in the Actions List

	7.0	6.0	5.5	IR7	IR3
	■	■	■	■	□

Both: Shift + click

Play an Action

	7.0	6.0	5.5	IR7	IR3
	■	■	■	■	■

Menu: Actions→Play

Mac: Cmd + double-click action

Win: Ctrl + double-click action

Both: Click the Play button

Play Just a Single Step of an Action

	7.0	6.0	5.5	IR7	IR3
	■	■	■	■	■

Mac: Cmd + double-click step

Win: Ctrl + double-click step

Both: (Cmd-click) the Play button; [Ctrl + click] the Play button

Actions

Toggle an Action Step On/Off

7.0 6.0 5.5 IR7 IR3

Both: Click Checkmark icon area

Toggle All Other Action Steps On/Off for This Action

7.0 6.0 5.5 IR7 IR3

Mac: Option + click the Checkmark icon area

Win: Alt + click the Checkmark icon area

Toggle Dialogs for an Action Step On/Off

7.0 6.0 5.5 IR7 IR3

Both: Click the Dialog icon area

You may not be able to do this—some commands must show a dialog, in which case the dialog icon will appear grayed out and cannot be toggled. Other commands can never present a dialog—menu commands like Select All, Deselect, etc.—so there won't be a dialog icon to toggle.

Toggle Dialogs for All Steps of an Action On/Off

7.0	6.0	5.5	IR7	IR3
■	■	■	■	■

Both: Click the Dialog icon area next to name of action

Toggle All Commands for a Set of Actions On/Off

7.0	6.0	5.5	IR7	IR3
■	■	■	■	□

Both: Click the Checkmark icon area for set

Toggle All Dialogs for a Set of Actions On/Off

7.0	6.0	5.5	IR7	IR3
■	■	■	■	□

Both: Click the Dialog icon area for set

Edit Command Options in an Action

7.0	6.0	5.5	IR7	IR3
■	■	■	■	■

Both: Double-click item

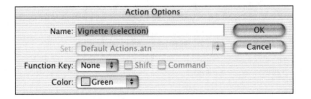

Create New Action

7.0	6.0	5.5	IR7	IR3
■	■	■	■	■

Menu: Action Palette→New Action

Both: Click the New Action button

Create New Action and Skip the Dialog Box

7.0	6.0	5.5	IR7	IR3
■	■	■	■	■

Mac: Option + click the New Action button

Win: Alt + click the New Action button

Actions

View/Hide All Steps of All Actions in a Set

7.0   6.0   5.5   IR7   IR3

■   ■   ■   ■   ☐

Mac: Option + click the triangle next to the set name

Win: Alt + click the triangle next to the set name

Toggle Dialogs for All Other Steps of an Action On/Off

7.0   6.0   5.5   IR7   IR3

■   ■   ■   ■   ☐

Mac: Option + click the Dialog icon area next to the step you want to leave on

Win: Alt + click the Dialog icon area next to the step you want to leave on

Actions

Best-Kept Secrets

After you've mastered the Top 15 tips on pages 1–4, you'll want to take a whack at Photoshop's best-kept secrets. These are the ones that will make novice users bow down in awe before you, chanting in unison, "I didn't know you could do *that!*" Maybe you already know some of them, but I guarantee that at least one of these puppies will catch your fancy. In no particular order, here they are:

1. Zoom In or Zoom Out: (Cmd + Plus)[Ctrl + Plus] or (Cmd + Minus)[Ctrl + Minus]

   These work even better with the plus and minus keys on the numeric keypad—they're easier to find without looking at the keyboard. This shortcut works to zoom the image while you have a dialog box onscreen.

2. Reposition a selection as you create it: Spacebar

   This one will save you so many steps, you'll wonder how you ever made selections before you knew it. Just don't let go of the mouse button while you're pressing on the spacebar, or the selection will be completed—then you can move it, but not continue to resize it.

3. Draw from the center while creating selections: (Option + drag)[Alt + drag]

   It seems simple and obvious after you try it, and it's particularly useful for elliptical selections. Trying to judge where the "corner" of an elliptical selection will fall is nearly impossible—and now you don't have to.

4. Paint or draw in a straight line: Shift + click

   So you can't draw a straight line—so what? Click once with any painting tool at the beginning of the line, and then Shift + click at the end of the line. Voilà! A straight line.

5. Cycle through open documents: Ctrl + Tab.

6. Create a protractor: (Option + drag)[Alt + drag] an end point of the measure tool's measure line.

   The angle change shows up in the Info palette.

7. Create a duplicate while transforming: (Cmd + Option + T) [Ctrl + Alt + T]

This shortcut is great when you're placing multiple, slightly different copies of an element throughout a document. You can do anything you want to the copy—resize it, rotate it, skew it, move it, whatever—without changing the original. If you have an active selection, you get a duplicate of the same layer. If you do not have a selection, you get a duplicate layer.

8. Fade the last filter used: (Cmd + Shift + F)[Ctrl + Shift + F]

Filter didn't come out right? Don't undo it—fade it. You can change the opacity and the blend mode of any filter, previewing your changes as you make them.

9. Reapply the last filter used: (Cmd + F)[Ctrl + F]

Why waste time looking for that filter in Photoshop's mare's nest of a Filter menu? If you're applying the same filter repeatedly, to one image or to many, just use this shortcut and take an early coffee break.

10. Transforming linked layers

If you want to scale, rotate, or otherwise transform more than one layer at a time, you can link the layers. When you use the Free Transform (Cmd + T)[Ctrl + T] in versions before Photoshop 7, even though you only see a bounding box around the contents of the active layer, you will be modifying all the linked layers simultaneously. In Photoshop 7, it is more obvious that you will be transforming all the linked layers because you see a bounding box that encloses all the linked layers.

11. Toggle the Airbrush mode On/Off

In Photoshop 7, there is no longer an Airbrush "tool." Rather, it is now a "mode" for any of the painting tools. Instead of clicking on the Airbrush mode icon in the Options bar when a painting tool is selected, you can press (Option + Shift + P)[Alt + Shift + P] instead.

Index

layers, 95
light, Lighting Effects
Preview, 163
dust from images, removing, 55

E

edge contrast, adjusting
Magnetic Lasso tool, 140
Magnetic Pen tool, 156
Edge Highlighter tool (Extract tool), 158
Edge Touchup tool (Extract tool), 158
Edit menu commands
Color Settings, 69
Fill, 74-76
Redo, 4, 23, 71
Transform, Numeric, 102-103, 138
Undo, 4, 71
editing
Action commands, 179
brushes, 47
colors, 89
master hue/saturation color range, 89
numeric entry values in dialog boxes, 57
pop-up sliders, 57
effects, layer effects
clearing, 116
hiding, 117
Effects, Clear Effects command (Layer menu), 115
embedding saved settings in Actions, 176
Eraser tool (Extract tool), 158
Exclusion (Blend mode), 50, 100
Extract command (Filter menu), 158
Extract tool, 158
reversing behavior, 158

Eyedropper tool
Extract tool, 158
toggling, 40, 120

F

fading filters, 182
last used, 157
Feather command (Select menu), 130
fields, Zoom Percentage Field, 51
File Browser, 63-64
File menu commands
Browse, 63
Close, 64
Close All, 64
Image Info, 66
Jump To, 67
New, 61
Open, 62
Page Setup, 66
Preferences, 68, 79
Preferences, Display & Cursors, 70
Preview In Browser, 67
Print, 66
Print One Copy, 67
Print Options, 66
Print Preview, 67
Print with Preview, 67
Quit, 68
Revert, 4, 65
Save, 64
Save a Copy, 65
Save As, 64
Save for Web, 65
Save Optimized, 65
Save Optimized As, 65
files
browsing when opening, 63-64
closing, 64
creating, 61
dragging between, centering while, 138
opening, 62-63
printing, 66-67

www.informit.com

YOUR GUIDE TO IT REFERENCE

New Riders has partnered with **InformIT.com** to bring technical information to your desktop. Drawing from New Riders authors and reviewers to provide additional information on topics of interest to you, **InformIT.com** provides free, in-depth information you won't find anywhere else.

Articles

Keep your edge with thousands of free articles, in-depth features, interviews, and IT reference recommendations—all written by experts you know and trust.

Online Books

Answers in an instant from **InformIT Online Books'** 600+ fully searchable online books.

POWERED BY

Safari

Catalog

Review online sample chapters, author biographies, and customer rankings and choose exactly the right book from a selection of over 5,000 titles.

New Riders

www.newriders.com

Publishing the Voices that Matter

OUR AUTHORS

PRESS ROOM

| web development | design | photoshop | new media | 3-D | server technologies |

EDUCATORS

ABOUT US

CONTACT US

You already know that New Riders brings you the **Voices that Matter**. But what does that mean? It means that New Riders brings you the Voices that challenge your assumptions, take your talents to the next level, or simply help you better understand the complex technical world we're all navigating.

Visit **www.newriders.com** to find:

- ▸ **10% discount** and **free shipping** on all book purchases
- ▸ Never-before-published chapters
- ▸ Sample chapters and excerpts
- ▸ Author bios and interviews
- ▸ Contests and enter-to-wins
- ▸ Up-to-date industry event information
- ▸ Book reviews
- ▸ Special offers from our friends and partners
- ▸ Info on how to join our User Group program
- ▸ Ways to have your Voice heard

WWW.NEWRIDERS.CO

HOW TO CONTACT US

VISIT OUR WEB SITE

WWW.NEWRIDERS.COM

On our web site, you'll find information about our other books, authors, tables of contents, and book errata. You will also find information about book registration and how to purchase our books, both domestically and internationally.

EMAIL US

Contact us at: **nrfeedback@newriders.com**

- If you have comments or questions about this book
- To report errors that you have found in this book
- If you have a book proposal to submit or are interested in writing for New Riders
- If you are an expert in a computer topic or technology and are interested in being a technical editor who reviews manuscripts for technical accuracy

Contact us at: **nreducation@newriders.com**

- If you are an instructor from an educational institution who wants to preview New Riders books for classroom use. Email should include your name, title, school, department, address, phone number, office days/hours, text in use, and enrollment, along with your request for desk/examination copies and/or additional information.

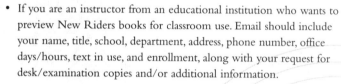

Contact us at: **nrmedia@newriders.com**

- If you are a member of the media who is interested in reviewing copies of New Riders books. Send your name, mailing address, and email address, along with the name of the publication or Web site you work for.

BULK PURCHASES/CORPORATE SALES

The publisher offers discounts on this book when ordered in quantity for bulk purchases and special sales. For sales within the U.S., please contact: Corporate and Government Sales (800) 382-3419 or **corpsales@pearsontechgroup.com**. Outside of the U.S., please contact: International Sales (317) 581-3793 or **international@pearsontechgroup.com**.

WRITE TO US

New Riders Publishing
201 W. 103rd St.
Indianapolis, IN 46290-1097

CALL/FAX US

Toll-free (800) 571-5840
If outside U.S. (317) 581-3500
Ask for New Riders
FAX: (317) 581-4663

New Riders

WWW.NEWRIDERS.COM

VOICES THAT MATTER

PHOTOSHOP® 7

**Photoshop 7
Down & Dirty Tricks**
Scott Kelby
0735712379
$39.99

Photoshop 7 Magic
Sherry London,
Rhoda Grossman
0735712646
$45.00

Photoshop 7 Artistry
Barry Haynes,
Wendy Crumpler
0735712409
$55.00

Photoshop 7 Killer Tips
Scott Kelby, Felix Nelson
0735713006
$39.99

Inside Photoshop 7
Gary Bouton, Barbara Bouton,
Robert Stanley, J. Scott Hamlin,
Daniel Will-Harris,
Mara Nathanson
0735712417
$49.99

**Photoshop Studio with
Bert Monroy**
Bert Monroy
0735712468
$45.00

**Photoshop
Restoration and Retouching**
Katrin Eisemann
0789723182
$49.99

**Photoshop Type Effects
Visual Encyclopedia**
Roger Pring
0735711909
$45.00

**Creative Thinking in
Photoshop**
Sharon Steuer
0735711224
$45.00

VOICES

THAT MATTEI